THE UNITED NATIONS
IN THE 21ST CENTURY

OTHER BOOKS BY DOUGLAS ROCHE

The Catholic Revolution (McKay, 1968)

Man to Man (Bruce, 1969) (With Bishop Remi De Roo)

It's A New World (Western Catholic Reporter, 1970)

Justice Not Charity: A New Global Ethic for Canada (McClelland & Stewart, 1976)

The Human Side of Politics (Clarke, Irwin, 1976)

What Development Is All About: China, Indonesia, Bangladesh (NC Press, 1979)

Politicians for Peace (NC Press, 1983)

United Nations: Divided World (NC Press, 1984)

Building Global Security: Agenda for the 1990s (NC Press, 1989)

In the Eye of the Catholic Storm (HarperCollins, 1992) (With Bishop Remi De Roo and Mary Jo Leddy)

A Bargain for Humanity: Global Security By 2000 (University of Alberta Press, 1993)

Safe Passage into the Twenty-First Century: The United Nations' Quest for Peace, Equality, Justice and Development (Continuum, 1995) (with Robert Muller)

An Unacceptable Risk: Nuclear Weapons in a Volatile World (Project Ploughshares, 1995)

The Ultimate Evil: The Fight to Ban Nuclear Weapons (Lorimer, 1997)

Bread Not Bombs: A Political Agenda for Social Justice (University of Alberta Press, 1999)

The Human Right to Peace (Novalis, 2003)

Beyond Hiroshima (Novalis, 2005)

Global Conscience (Novalis, 2007)

Creative Dissent: A Politician's Struggle for Peace (Novalis, 2008)

How We Stopped Loving the Bomb (Lorimer, 2011)

Peacemakers: How people around the world are building a world free of war (Lorimer, 2014)

THE UNITED NATIONS
IN THE 21ST CENTURY

Grappling with the world's most challenging issues:
militarism, the environment, human rights, inequality

DOUGLAS ROCHE

JAMES LORIMER & COMPANY LTD., PUBLISHERS
TORONTO

James Lorimer & Company Ltd., Publishers acknowledges the support of the Ontario Arts Council. We acknowledge the support of the Canada Council for the Arts which last year invested $24.3 million in writing and publishing throughout Canada. We acknowledge the Government of Ontario through the Ontario Media Development Corporation's Ontario Book Initiative.

Cover design: Meredith Bangay
Cover image: iStock

Library and Archives Canada Cataloguing in Publication

Roche, Douglas, 1929-, author
The United Nations in the 21st century / Douglas Roche.

Includes bibliographical references and index.
Issued in print and electronic formats.
ISBN 978-1-4594-0949-1 (paperback).--ISBN 978-1-4594-0950-7 (epub)

1. United Nations. 2. Security, International. 3. Global warming.
4. Human rights. I. Title.

JZ4984.5.R63 2015   341.23   C2015-904215-1
                                            C2015-904216-X

James Lorimer & Company Ltd., Publishers
317 Adelaide Street West, Suite 1002
Toronto, ON, Canada
M5V 1P9
www.lorimer.ca

Printed and bound in Canada.

In memory of Dag Hammarskjöld, 1905-1961,
whose courageous leadership of the United Nations
has inspired me through the years

CONTENTS

INTRODUCTION
THE UNITED NATIONS AND PEACE: A FAIR ASSESSMENT

One view of the world today sees chaos everywhere. Not since the end of the World War II have there been so many refugees, displaced people, and asylum seekers. Extremism and nationalism are on the rise. Terrorist groups, such as the Islamic State and Boko Haram, have seized large territories, committed gross human rights violations, and triggered humanitarian crises. Atrocities, the deliberate starvation of civilians, and assaults on hospitals and shelters have become common. The suffering of women and children in failed states is unendurable. Diplomacy among different regions and cultures is on the defensive, undermined by spates of violence in the Middle East and Africa.

Another view is that, despite the problems highlighted in the news every day, the world as a whole is moving to a higher stage of civilization. All the big indicators of modern life — health, education, commerce, science, energy, shipping, communications, transportation, law, women's rights — are expanding. Two billion people in Africa, Asia, and Latin America have been lifted out of dire poverty in the past two decades. A new global middle class is emerging. More people can claim their human rights than ever before. The major powers are not fighting one another as they did in the twentieth century.

Which is the real world? Both these views reflect reality. So how are we to make sense of such divergence and how can we build hope for an enduring peace?

In four decades in public life as a parliamentarian, ambassador, and civil society activist, I have been preoccupied with this question. I find myself repeatedly coming back to the United Nations, the only place where 193 nations come together to work out, in six languages, their global problems. The UN was started seventy years ago "to save succeeding generations from the scourge of war." How successful is it?

At one level, the UN's record of accomplishments is astonishing. It delivers food to 90 million people in eighty countries, assists 38 million refugees, protects human rights through eighty treaties and declarations, deploys 120,000 personnel in sixteen peacekeeping missions, in addition to thirteen political and peacebuilding missions which are averting future genocides. The UN is responsible for aviation safety, detecting global warming, and rising literacy rates among the world's poorest. It is charting the seas and space as the common property of humanity.

At another level, the UN is criticized for its failures — it hasn't stopped the slaughter of innocent people in Syria and Iraq, and there are still millions of destitute people. Speeches without end are made at the green marble podium in the General Assembly and float off into the atmosphere. When international tensions mount, the big powers frequently bypass the very body they built to guarantee security.

In looking at the sprawling organization headquartered in New York, with branches in Geneva, Vienna, Nairobi, and outposts in virtually every country, I have asked myself a basic question: Is the United Nations effective in building human security? The pillars of human security are arms control and disarmament, sustainable economic and social development, environmental protection, and the advancement of human rights. That is the agenda of peace. How successful is the United Nations in developing that agenda?

That is the question I set out to answer in this book. The answer is vital in trying to make sense of the conflicting trends on the world scene today. Can the twenty-first century be a time of peace, or are we mired in the muck of hatred? The United Nations is trying to lift up humanity, to show that over the horizon clearer waters are ahead. At its seventieth anniversary, it is time for the UN's human security work to be fairly presented, not with a cheerleading hurrah, but with a level-headed assessment of how the organization affects the life of every person on the planet.

CHAPTER ONE
AVERTING WORLD WAR III

At 2:30 p.m. on October 24, 1962, Acting Secretary-General U Thant, sitting at his desk on the 38th floor of United Nations headquarters in New York, sent an urgent message to Soviet Premier Nikita Khrushchev and US President John F. Kennedy, appealing for a moratorium to halt further action in the Cuban Missile Crisis. Thant, a Burmese diplomat, had suddenly been thrust into the UN's top job the year before, when his predecessor Dag Hammarskjöld was killed in a plane crash in Africa en route to negotiate a truce in the Congolese civil war. Even though Thant had not been confirmed as secretary-general, he realized he had to act. His action to defuse an explosive crisis by using the authority of his UN office has never been given the historical acclaim it deserves.

At first, both Kennedy and Khrushchev reacted negatively and were even hostile to Thant for proposing that — in order to end the crisis caused by the Soviets secretly sending nuclear arms to Cuba — the Soviets must voluntarily suspend shipments and the United States lift the naval quarantine it had imposed.

Thant made his message public. Tensions rose through the night as cables flew back and forth between Washington, Moscow, and New York.

Suddenly, Kennedy saw a way for the Soviets to stop their shipments without looking like they had capitulated to the United States. He asked Thant to send a second message to Khrushchev stating that if the Soviets would hold up shipments, the United States "would be glad to get into conversations about how the situation could be adjusted." Meanwhile in Moscow, Khrushchev was also having second thoughts about the value of Thant's first message and sent the secretary-general a cable stating that he accepted the UN intervention, "which is in the interest of peace."

Diplomacy was moving fast and Thant stepped up the pressure. On October 25, at 2:26 p.m., just before the Security Council took up the issue at what became one of the most famous UN meetings ever held, Thant sent out his second set of appeals. He asked Khrushchev to instruct Soviet vessels en route to Cuba to stay away from the quarantine area; he simultaneously asked Kennedy to instruct US vessels to avoid direct confrontation with Soviet ships. To both leaders, he stated, "This would permit discussions of the modalities of a possible agreement which could settle the problem peacefully."

Down in the Security Council chamber, US Ambassador Adlai Stevenson confronted Soviet Ambassador Valerian Zorin with photographic evidence of the placement of Soviet missiles in Cuba. Stevenson thundered: "Do you, Ambassador Zorin, deny that the USSR has placed and is placing medium- and intermediate-range missiles and sites in Cuba? Yes or no — don't wait for the translation — yes or no?" When Zorin refused to answer, Stevenson's blistering attack ricocheted around the world: "I am prepared to wait for my answer until hell freezes over."

The public and backroom negotiations intensified. On October 27, *The New York Times* blared: "UN Talks Open: Soviet Agrees to Shun Blockade Zone Now." The crisis ended a few days later when Khrushchev agreed to verifiably remove his missiles from Cuba in return for a United States non-invasion pledge. There was also a deal, kept secret at the time, in which Kennedy agreed to decommission aging US Jupiter missiles from Turkey six months later. Thant, who had been keeping in touch privately with Cuba's leader, Fidel Castro, flew to Cuba to try to establish a UN mission to ensure no further work would be done on the nuclear sites. But a humiliated Castro refused to permit entry to UN inspectors. American and Soviet negotiators, meeting regularly at the UN headquarters over the next few weeks, completed the process of getting the missiles out of Cuba.

This diplomatic manoeuvring became the UN's finest hour. Had the United States and the Soviet Union not come to a negotiated settlement of the Cuban Missile Crisis, there is little doubt that World War III would have begun, with nuclear missiles raining down on the American and Russian populations. It would have been a catastrophe of epic proportions. Fortunately for the world, both Kennedy and Khrushchev seized the opening Thant had provided. When it was over, the United States and Soviet governments sent a letter to Thant expressing, in diplomatic understatement, "appreciation for your efforts in assisting our Governments to avert the serious threat to peace which recently arose in the Caribbean area." President Kennedy added his own note of praise: "U Thant has put the world deeply in his debt."

Though Thant's intervention was the crucial act in resolving the crisis, the American government took the credit. Secretary of State Dean Rusk told the media, "We were eyeball to eyeball and the other guy blinked." In other words, all this had been a game of nuclear chicken. The American public loved it. Thant, never a showman, returned to his duties.

ROOSEVELT STARTED UN

Thant's decisive involvement in the Cuban Missile Crisis came at a time when the prestige of the United Nations was still at the high point it enjoyed from its birth in 1945. The American government and people, except for a small band of hardcore isolationists, loved the UN. Their affection stemmed from the faith that two of their presidents, Roosevelt and Truman, put in the organization even before the UN Charter was adopted in San Francisco on June 26, 1945.

Without the extraordinary vision of President Franklin D. Roosevelt, the United Nations would never have originated. In the darkest days of World War II, Roosevelt sold the idea of a permanent body of states to avert future wars to his war-time allies, British Prime Minister Winston Churchill and Soviet Premier Josef Stalin. The failure of the League of Nations, started after World War I, was fresh in everyone's minds. But Roosevelt persisted and assembled a team to start writing a charter for the new organization.

When he died suddenly on April 12, 1945, plans were well advanced for the launching of the organization at a conference in San Francisco only a few weeks later. The advisors of Harry Truman, who, as vice-president, succeeded Roosevelt, tried to persuade the new president to postpone the event to give himself more time. But Truman was just as enthusiastic as Roosevelt and ordered the conference to proceed on schedule. When all the deliberations had finished, Truman flew to San Francisco for the final plenary session and proclaimed: "Oh, what a great day this can be for history."

The battles over the charter, composition of the membership, and rights given to the Security Council were blistering. Fifty-one

countries were admitted as original members. Eleven (now fifteen) of them were given seats on the Security Council, which was
charged under the Charter with "primary responsibility for the
maintenance of international peace and security." The major powers — the United States, the Soviet Union (now Russia), the United
Kingdom, France, and China — gave themselves permanent seats
on the Council and the power to veto any substantive resolution,
an act criticized to this day. The veto provision has been used 234
times (mostly by the former Soviet Union and now Russia and
the United States) since the UN officially came into existence on
October 24, 1945. There is no doubt it gives these states unwarranted power, but it is virtually certain that, fearing that any one of
them could be overwhelmed by a vote forcing them into unwanted
action, they would not have joined without it. On the other hand,
because Security Council resolutions are binding with the power of
international law, they take on great weight with the power of the
permanent five members (P5) united behind them.

The United States, continuing to display a dynamic faith in
the organization, agreed to pay 25 per cent (now 22 per cent) of the
organization's bills. John D. Rockefeller, the American financier,
donated the land on which the UN headquarters in Manhattan
stands. At first, there was a reasonable amount of harmony. The
General Assembly's first resolution established a commission "to
deal with the problems raised by the discovery of atomic energy."
But the United States and Soviet distrust of each other, never far
beneath the surface in the negotiations over the Charter, burst out
into the open as each side struggled to maintain superiority in the
burgeoning nuclear arms race. The UN, still in its cradle, had to
contend with the new Cold War.

Secretary-General Dag Hammarskjöld became the leading
diplomat in the world, respected by East and West as he tried

to contain small wars in Africa. Shortly after his sudden death, President Kennedy, paying tribute to him in the General Assembly, said the UN was "the only true alternative to war."

COOPERATION LOST AS WORLD CHANGED

Though the Security Council was often paralyzed, UN peacekeeping, started in the Suez in 1956, was beginning to take hold. The mood was bright in 1961. Kennedy and Khrushchev authorized their principal arms control negotiators, John M. McCloy and Valerian Zorin, to negotiate a framework for comprehensive disarmament. In five months, the American and Soviet teams produced a document, known as the McCloy–Zorin principles, which committed the two superpowers to negotiate an agreement to "ensure that disarmament is general and complete and war is no longer an instrument for settling international problems." Arms would be reduced, in a reliable and verified way, to the level needed to maintain internal order. In addition, they agreed to "support and provide agreed manpower for a United Nations peace force." The framework document, agreed to by both the United States and the Soviet Union, was unanimously endorsed by the General Assembly.

But cooperation dwindled as the world changed dramatically in the 1960s. President Kennedy was assassinated, as were his brother Robert Kennedy and Martin Luther King Jr. The mood turned downward in the United States as the Vietnam War escalated, the UN's de-colonization processes brought into the organization many small states with new demands, and the clamour of the "developing" countries for economic equity grew louder.

In the early 1970s, the UN, with non-aligned states — those in neither the Soviet nor American spheres of influence — now in a majority, took an action that tarnished its reputation in the West. With growing Arab membership and the Palestine Liberation

Organization granted observer status, the General Assembly adopted a resolution that determined "Zionism is a form of racism and racial discrimination." The non-aligned states insisted that the displacement of Palestinians, and Israel's refusal to allow refugees to return, violated UN principles, but key Western states held that the resolution questioned Israel's very legitimacy. The resolution was rescinded in 1991, but not before poisoning relations between some Western states and much of the rest of the UN. Tempers also flared when the developing countries began to push back at what they considered an economic stranglehold maintained by the World Bank and the International Monetary Fund, the UN's chief financial instruments. OPEC's big jump in oil prices in 1973 sent shivers down the spines of Western leaders, who were now becoming fearful that their control over the UN's direction was being challenged.

By the 1980s and the election of Ronald Reagan on a right-wing wave, United States' disenchantment with the UN set in. Critics painted the UN as an anti-Western, Third-World club. They began to characterize the UN as, in US Senator Daniel Patrick Moynihan's phrase, "tyranny of the majority," which described how the new nations were regularly outvoting the West. Reagan's ambassador to the UN, Jeane J. Kirkpatrick, conveniently forgetting the United States possessed a veto preventing the Security Council from doing anything the United States didn't like, complained that the American position is "essentially impotent, without influence, heavily outvoted, and isolated." One of her associate ambassadors, Charles Lichenstein, shocked the assembly by declaring that the UN ought to get out of the United States, insultingly adding: "We will be at the dockside bidding you farewell." This broadside was made worse by Reagan stating that Lichenstein's remarks reflected the feelings of most Americans.

Congress began delaying payment of the United States' dues to the UN, crippling the organization's ability to do sound planning. For years, this sourness went on and probably reached its peak when US Secretary of State Madeleine Albright, piqued that Secretary-General Boutros Boutros-Ghali had answered her claim that the United States was the "indispensable nation" by saying the UN was the "indispensable organization," convinced President Bill Clinton to veto Boutros-Ghali's second term.

When Clinton withdrew American troops from a peace-keeping mission in Somalia in 1994 after the American people expressed outrage at photos of dead US soldiers being dragged through the streets of Mogadishu, the UN suffered another set-back. The harrowing images were a significant factor in Clinton's reluctance to have the UN put a strengthened military force into Rwanda to stop the genocide in which 800,000 people were killed in 100 days.

The mass slaughter of Tutsi and moderate Hutu in Rwanda by the Hutu majority was the worst atrocity since the Holocaust of World War II. The Canadian general, Roméo Dallaire, commanding a small UN peacekeeping force on the ground, appealed in vain to headquarters for a stronger contingent. Later, after becoming secretary-general in 1997, Kofi Annan acknowledged the failure of the UN and the international community in Rwanda: "The international community and the UN could not muster the political will to confront [the evil]. The world must deeply repent this failure."

Tragically, another UN failure followed Rwanda. Although the Security Council had declared Srebrenica a "safe area" in the Bosnian War, Bosnian Serb forces massacred 7,000 Muslim boys and men and expelled 20,000 civilians in a crime of "ethnic cleansing." Years later, a civil court in The Hague found Dutch UN peacekeepers guilty of turning over hundreds of Bosnian Muslim men over to Serb forces, who then slaughtered them. Again Annan wrote: "Through error, misjudgement and an inability to recognize the scope of the evil confronting us, we failed to do our part to help save the people of Srebrenica from the [Bosnian] Serb campaign of mass murder."

RECOVERING ITS STRENGTH

The crucible of Rwanda and Srebrenica proved a turning point for the UN. Under Annan's decisive leadership, tribunals were established to convict and punish the guilty, the International Criminal Court was formed, a high-level panel led by the distinguished Algerian diplomat, Lakhdar Brahimi, set new standards for peacekeeping in the post–Cold War era, a new approach to peacebuilding was developed and, most importantly, the Responsibility to Protect doctrine adopted. As well, the Millennium Development Goals to eradicate the worst forms of poverty were established.

All this work, which I will describe in greater detail in later chapters, lifted up the UN and set it on a new trajectory. The clumsiness and uncertainty of UN efforts have been replaced with a greater sense of confidence that the organization can indeed build the conditions for peace in the world — even if the selfish interests of the P5 still hold back strong collective action. Kofi Annan was awarded the Nobel Peace Prize for his leadership, and this honour may well have given him the strength to state — to the chagrin of the Bush Administration — that the 2003 US War in Iraq was "illegal" because it was not authorized by the Security Council.

Under Ban Ki-moon, who became secretary-general in 2007 after serving as South Korea's foreign minister, the UN has settled down and regained its stability. It is not as dynamic as some would want, but its critics have trouble faulting it. When President Barack

Obama chaired the unprecedented Security Council summit on nuclear weapons in 2009, the full involvement of the United States in using the UN to deal with the greatest threat to human security was on dramatic display. It was a striking illustration of the confidence the UN has regained from the American government and people. A 2013 global survey by Pew Research showed 58 per cent of Americans have a favourable view of the UN, an increase since Obama's election. The favourable rating was almost twice the 31 per cent of Americans who disfavoured the UN.

Pew surveyed 39 countries and found a median favourable rating of 58 per cent. In Russia, however, the favourable rating was only 28 per cent with 53 per cent of Russians dissatisfied. The UN, it seems, still has a lot of work to do to prove itself to all the world's people.

CHAPTER TWO
THE UN VS. MILITARISM

What is the single biggest obstacle preventing the United Nations from fulfilling the goals of the Charter?

Is it the veto system in the Security Council, a lack of vision, or ineptness of officials? No. What holds back the UN is the constant militarism driving the policies of almost all states.

By militarism, I mean the exaltation of military values in the resolution of conflict, which leads to aggressive readiness to use military means to resolve conflict and downplaying the possibilities of diplomatic resolution. The quick recourse to bombing in the crises in Kosovo, Afghanistan, and Iraq all were incited by militarist thinking that ignored, in the heat of the moment, the possibility that the UN mechanisms might restore peace. The bombing campaign against Islamist extremists in Syria and Iraq swept by the possibility that a UN force, authorized by the Security Council, could have produced an effective and humanitarian containment of extremism.

Militarism feeds a culture of war, and the greatest contributors to this thinking are the powerful figures driving the military-industrial complex. Just before leaving office in 1961, US President Dwight Eisenhower, a World War II hero, cautioned his fellow citizens about the growing unwarranted influence of the "permanent armaments industry of vast proportions." He warned: "The potential for the disastrous rise of misplaced power exists and will persist." Unfortunately, his warning went unheeded and the arms corporations multiplied, spawning an insidious system which finances the election campaigns of untold numbers of legislators, some of whom become arms lobbyists themselves when they leave office.

Seven of the top ten arms producers in the world are American. The United States accounts for more than 40 per cent of the $1.7 trillion annual military spending in the world. In 2014, the Congressional Budget Office reported that the United States will spend $355 billion on nuclear weapons in the next decade. President Obama won the Nobel Peace Prize for a speech committing the United States "to seek the peace and security of a world without nuclear weapons," but he appears acquiescent to the Pentagon drive to ensure that nuclear weapons become normalized and a permanent part of the twenty-first-century American arsenal.

While the United States spending figures stand out, the total spending of all nine nuclear weapons states on their nuclear arsenals in the next decade will exceed $1 trillion. Militarism has run amuck. These national policies violate both morality and common sense. These weapons cannot be used without violating the basic precepts of international humanitarian law, but also their cost is siphoning money desperately needed to meet the education, health, and social demands of burgeoning populations.

To quote President Eisenhower again: "Every gun that is made, every warship launched, every rocket fired signifies, in the final sense, a theft from those who hunger and are not fed, those who are cold and not clothed." He said this in the early days of his presidency, but not even the power of the White House could slow down arms spending. Every president and indeed every leader of a major country is encircled by the greedy and powerful arms merchants. No spending is ever enough for the military-industrial complex. The arms merchants have forced governments to make a mockery of Article 26 of the Charter, which calls for peace and security "with the least diversion for armaments of the world's human and economic resources."

EFFORTS TO OVERCOME MILITARISM

When Mikhail Gorbachev assumed the leadership of the Soviet Union in the dying days of the Cold War, he came to the General Assembly in New York with a sweeping presentation of world reform to get rid of militarism. World progress, he said, is only possible through a search for universal human consensus. His renunciation of force won vigorous applause: ". . . the use or threat of force no longer can or must be an instrument of foreign policy. This applies above all to nuclear arms." Pledging unilateral troop reductions and withdrawal of divisions from Eastern Europe, he called for a range of new international institutions to strengthen the UN: a multilateral centre for lessening the dangers of war, an international verification mechanism under UN auspices, a tribunal to investigate acts of terrorism, a special fund for humanitarian cooperation, and a world space organization. The delegates cheered for ten minutes. But Gorbachev lost power when the Soviet Union dissolved in 1991. The momentary cooperation with the United States did not last, and the oligarchs came into their own in Russia.

When Indian Prime Minister Rajiv Ghandi presented a fifteen-year action plan for the total elimination of nuclear weapons to a UN special session on disarmament, the Western states gave him the back of their hand. Militarism — in this case, the idea that maintaining their stocks was vital to the credibility of nuclear deterrence — drove their thinking. India later joined the nuclear club and so did Pakistan. Israel acquired nuclear weapons. The militarists in countries around the world would not be denied, even with the demise of the Cold War.

When the Cold War ended, many people thought that the world would get a "peace dividend." No such luck. Arms spending continued to climb through the 1990s, with local wars breaking out in parts of Europe, Africa, and Asia. When the terrorists of 9/11 struck and fear became the new common denominator of government policies, militarism rose to new levels. Spending on conventional weapons mushroomed. The UN, trying to get both political and financial support for its new peacebuilding programs, was shoved aside.

Despite the culture of war thinking, which still governs many chancelleries, the UN has succeeded in raising the level of understanding of what constitutes the real basis of security in a globalized world. Security today is not just the protection of national borders but the guarantee that humans can develop their lives free of violence and the ravages of destitution.

That has been one of the organization's major accomplishments, for it is responding to the major challenge of our era: the humanitarian crisis brought on by this transformational moment in world history. The spread of individual human rights in the twenty-first century is clashing against centuries-old militarist thinking that all power comes from a gun. The UN Charter opens with the words "We the peoples of the United Nations . . ." are determined to "save succeeding generations from the scourge of war," but it goes on to reaffirm "the dignity and worth of the human person." What may have been seen as a rhetorical flourish in 1945 is being taken seriously today.

An opening illustration of the new thinking was provided by the UN at the 1987 International Conference on the Relationship of Disarmament and Development. This UN meeting was the culmination of a three-year study of disarmament and development issues by twenty-seven world experts headed by the formidable Swedish diplomat Inga Thorsson. She argued that a "dynamic triangular relationship" links disarmament, development, and security. Security for all would be enhanced by vigorously pursuing disarmament and development in their own right. The conference pursued this theme and, although the Western countries refused to set up a development fund from monies saved by cutting back on arms, they did agree that all economies would be improved by curtailed military spending.

The UN continued to enlarge the meaning of security from the protection of a state to the protection of every individual. In 1992, Secretary-General Boutros Boutros-Ghali gave the Security Council a seminal document, *An Agenda for Peace*, which introduced an interplay of preventive diplomacy, peacemaking, and peacekeeping techniques to strengthen the UN's ability to identify and deal with potential crises. No longer would the UN just be responding to crises — though that would always be necessary, especially in dealing with natural disasters — it would also try to prevent disputes in early stages from becoming full-scale wars.

Boutros-Ghali tried to resurrect the idea, originally considered during the Charter negotiations five decades earlier, of a permanent UN peacekeeping force. He proposed that nations make available a contingent of one thousand troops capable of deployment on twenty-four hours' notice to incipient hot spots.

Fearing the implications of the UN having its own "army" interfering with the sovereignty of states, the major powers insisted that peacekeeping be restricted to an ad hoc basis even though it customarily takes several months to assemble a UN mission for deployment into the field.

THE START OF PEACEBUILDING

Despite these handicaps, the UN has, over the years, mounted sixty-nine peacekeeping and observer missions to the world's trouble spots, allowing many countries to at least stop recurrent conflict. Peacekeeping operations in Cambodia, El Salvador, Liberia, Mozambique, Namibia, and Sierra Leone stand out as success stories. UN peacekeeping was awarded the Nobel Peace Prize in 1988. There are currently sixteen peacekeeping operations around the world, staffed by 120,000 troops and other personnel from 122 countries. Current UN peacekeeping work in the Central African Republic and Mali has stopped the chaos in those places from turning into genocide.

Gradually, Boutros-Ghali's ideas about prevention began to take hold and the UN attempted to bring together all the elements of peacebuilding: political relationships, peacekeeping, development, humanitarianism, and human rights. The training of judges, monitoring of elections, and the development of stable government institutions were all rolled into a consolidated effort to bring relevant actors together. When Kofi Annan led the 2005 UN reform efforts, one of his innovations was a Peacebuilding Commission, which met with some success in reconstruction efforts in Burundi and Sierra Leone. However, little government financing and many stumbles over turf protection — as the many UN agencies involved argued over areas of responsibility — slowed down this work. Moreover, governments are not greatly attracted to shoring up fragile states where corruption, poor governance, and weak institutions keep spawning civil conflict.

Nevertheless, the Peacebuilding Commission represents a significant step forward to replace outmoded militarist thinking. Carolyn McAskie, a Canadian who was in charge of this work, says: "The effort . . . was founded on a belief that we all have a joint responsibility for ensuring the sustainability of global peace based on peace within individual countries and regions."

This peacemaking work of the UN has not received the credit it deserves for the 40 per cent decline in conflict around the world since the 1990s. UN preventive diplomacy and other forms of preventive action have defused many potential conflicts. Further, conflicts in some regions of Africa that might otherwise have escalated into future genocides have been defused by the ongoing work of the new UN Office for the Prevention of Genocide. Western publics don't hear about tragedies that never happen, so the absence of publicity compounds the UN's ability to generate financial support for preventive diplomacy.

Conflicts in Syria, Iraq, and the Middle East naturally draw big headlines. When the Security Council is paralyzed by wrangling and protecting client states, bloodshed occurs. But to claim that the UN is impotent in world crises completely misses the point that the "UN" can only enforce peace when the P5 allow it to.

When the P5 worked together in the Security Council to clear chemical weapons out of Syria, countless lives were saved. Also, the P5 cooperated to put in place a legal framework to combat terrorism. Fourteen global agreements have been negotiated under the leadership of the Security Council, including treaties against hostage-taking, aircraft hijacking, terrorist bombings, financing of terrorism, and nuclear terrorism. These treaties have contributed significantly to global security. Terrorism, of course, is still perceived as a common threat, but the threat could be considerably reduced if national governments more fully employed the multilateral machinery inaugurated by the UN.

THE RESPONSIBILITY TO PROTECT

Out of the limelight, the UN has fostered a unifying idea that goes far beyond the old dichotomy of disarmament and development; that is, peace and security come from the integration of development, disarmament, and human rights. This is far more complex than the old argument of guns versus butter. Also, the integration of policies gets away from the polarizing language of "North" and "South." In the new era, policies affecting climate, nuclear destruction, trade, finance, and other major issues jump across regions and affect everyone everywhere. No region, let alone country, can live in isolation. Cooperation is essential for mutual success. This is the basic idea underlying common security, a theme fleshed out in several UN conferences over the past twenty years.

The peacebuilding ideas gave birth in 2001 to the Responsibility to Protect (RtoP) doctrine, which has enabled the UN to make a big jump from its early days when protection of state security occupied most of the agenda. The slaughter of so many innocent people in Cambodia, Rwanda, Bosnia, the Central African Republic, and elsewhere awakened the consciences of many leaders into realizing that the protection of human beings had an equally compelling claim on international law.

A UN World Summit of 150 government leaders in 2005 unanimously endorsed the principle that people must be protected from genocide, war crimes, ethnic cleansing, and crimes against humanity. If states fail to protect their citizens from atrocities, and peaceful measures fail to bring improvements, then collective military action, under the authority of the Security Council, can be taken.

The most famous example of the use of RtoP was NATO's air war against Libya to protect civilians from massacre by Colonel Muammar Gaddafi. Fighters went on to capture and kill Gaddafi, a regime change that was not specifically called for in the Security Council's mandate for the operation. The strict containment of the Responsibility to Protect to help civilians and not to be used as an excuse to topple leaders is at the heart of a continuing controversy over the efficacy of RtoP. Although it has worked effectively in Mali, Ivory Coast, Guinea, and Kenya, some non-aligned countries see RtoP as a new form of imperialism.

The problems attached to humanitarian intervention are huge as are the obstacles to securing convictions at the International Criminal Court, set up to bring justice to victims of war crimes. The corruption infecting many political systems impedes the security sought by millions of oppressed people.

The strengthening of international law is at once the most challenging task of the UN and the greatest reason for hope for a more peaceful world. Over its seven decades, 560 multilateral treaties — on human rights, terrorism, global crime, refugees, disarmament, trade, commodities, the oceans, and many other subjects — have been achieved through UN efforts. The Arms Trade Treaty of 2013 regulates the $74 billion international trade in conventional arms. The UN has made us safer.

One great goal in the development of international law for human security remains elusive: a legal framework for the prohibition and elimination of nuclear weapons. It defies logic that the international community benefits from global treaties banning chemical and biological weapons, but is denied a treaty banning the worst form of weapons of mass destruction. Here the vicious hand of militarism is particularly blatant.

Secretary-General Ban has called for a nuclear weapons convention or a framework of legal instruments to eliminate all the remaining 16,300 nuclear weapons, the smallest of which carries more destructive power than the bomb that blew up Hiroshima. Three-quarters of the states at the UN have voted for the commencement of negotiations for a treaty. Countless civil society organizations are campaigning for a nuclear-weapons-free world. Pope Francis has spoken out. Former nuclear weapons defenders have reversed their opinions. Still, the P5, the major arms producers in the world, are holding out against a mounting call to head off the "catastrophic humanitarian consequences" of a nuclear explosion. They have arrogantly assumed that they can modernize their nuclear systems and retain them for the rest of the twenty-first century while proscribing their acquisition by other states.

At the very least "verifiable, legally binding and irreversible commitments on nuclear disarmament are required to achieve . . . a world free of nuclear weapons," said two former directors of the UN disarmament office, Jayantha Dhanapala of Sri Lanka and Sergio Duarte of Brazil, who have presided over review conferences of the Non-Proliferation Treaty. The continued refusal of the nuclear powers to give such legal commitments is now challenged by a groundswell of humanitarian rejection of nuclear weapons. The future ability of the United Nations to guarantee peace and security for all will depend on whether people power can at last overcome the deadly tentacles of militarism.

CHAPTER THREE
FROM CHARITY TO JUSTICE

In the early days of the UN, helping the destitute of the world through aid programs was largely seen as charity. If it would be too much to say that the Sustainable Development Goals, a complex intertwining of economic and social projects, launched by the UN in 2015, will produce social justice, at least "the road to dignity," in the words of Secretary-General Ban, has been opened up.

Praise for the UN's lifting two billion people out of poverty in the past twenty years is mitigated by the shocking fact that the richest one per cent of the world's population owns half of the world's wealth. Social justice in the world is a long way off.

Still, the UN's humanitarian work has definitely contributed to reducing the wealth inequality that blights modern civilization. Extreme poverty has been cut in half since 1990, an estimated 3.3 million deaths from malaria averted, 22 million lives saved from tuberculosis, and 6.6 million lives saved from HIV/AIDS. UNICEF's work with children has cut in half the number of deaths of those under five. Today, 91 per cent of children attend primary school, 84 per cent of adults can read, and the female literacy rate has climbed to nearly 80 per cent.

The UN Development Programme runs 4,800 projects in 170 countries. Some 60 million refugees fleeing persecution, violence, and war have been helped by the Office of the UN High Commissioner for Refugees. The International Fund for Agricultural Development provides low-interest loans and grants to rural people, helping 430 million women and men to grow and sell more food and increase their incomes. The UN Human Settlements Programme turns slums into decent housing settlements. A thirteen-year effort by the World Health Organization resulted in the complete eradication of smallpox from the planet in 1980, saving an estimated $1 billion a year in vaccination and monitoring.

The sheer number of people whose lives have been saved and strengthened by UN agencies would seem to justify the existence of the UN even if it did nothing else. This is not just statistics we are dealing with, rather it is the elevation of suffering people to freedom from want, a reasonable amount of control over their own lives, and the opportunity to live in violence-free surroundings. What kind of human beings would we be if we did not extend a helping hand to the destitute?

Of course, the UN's humanitarian work is vital. And those who scoff at international aid "going down the drain" are sadly uninformed. No system of the delivery of aid can be impregnable against corruption, but the failures are greatly outweighed by the magnitude of international aid unprecedented in world history. Thousands of UN aid workers risk their lives every day to carry out their tasks.

However, the UN was not meant to be a welfare agency, nor can its activities be confined thus. It was founded primarily to stop and avert wars. It is fundamentally a political body. The Security Council, the heart of the UN system, is supposed to maintain peace and security.

The founders did recognize that, in the pursuit of peace, economic conditions had to be strengthened. Thus, the Charter calls for "the creation of conditions of stability and well-being," through higher standards of living, full employment, and social progress and development. For this purpose, the Economic and Social Council was created. But its strength lies mainly in the studies it conducts on fairer trade and finance policies, not in action to cure poverty. The vast activity of the UN agencies deals with helping the victims of poverty, not in changing the economic system.

The Western states appear to be content when the UN alleviates human distress, but when resolutions are put forth, particularly by the non-aligned states, calling for equity in trade and finance regulations to get at the roots of the poverty problem, they bristle. When the General Assembly adopted a declaration on the Right to Development in 1986, stating that everyone is entitled to economic, social, cultural, and political development, the document languished on library shelves. Charity is fine. But the powerful states are not ready to embrace an equitable world order.

GLOBAL SHARING OF POWER

In the 1970s, developing countries, seeking to break the chain of economic dependence on the West, succeeded in having the UN adopt a declaration calling for a New International Economic Order to counter what they claimed was an unjust economic system that kept them in perpetual poverty. The newly formed Group of 77 called for a restructuring of the international economic system to allow them to share in the decision-making processes. They wanted global economic negotiations on such subjects as commodity agreements to improve and stabilize their export earnings on raw materials, liberalized trade, increased energy financing, greater attention by the International Monetary Fund and the World Bank to the debt and development needs of poor countries, and stepped up assistance to meet the UN target of 0.7 per cent of gross national product of the industrialized countries.

This "North–South" agenda became not just a question of economic progress but an issue of global sharing of power. The North, increasingly beset by recession and unemployment, was in no mood for sharing control over the financial, trading, and technology systems. This became clear at a North–South summit of twenty-two world leaders at Cancun, Mexico, in 1981, which produced debate but no action on negotiations.

The Cancun Summit stirred think tanks in many places. The following years saw a succession of independent commissions and UN world conferences that increasingly focused on a new understanding of common security. Although the term "common security" was first thought to apply to military matters, it soon started to be applied to economic and social development. Trading and monetary systems between and within North and South are interdependent. The South needs capital from the North. The North needs markets in the South. At first, the idea of common security was brushed aside, but when the world began to focus on environmental problems, which visibly leap across national borders, many governments began to realize they could not solve mounting social problems by themselves.

The UN held an Earth Summit in Rio de Janeiro in 1992, a gigantic gathering of states and civil society, which laid out a blueprint for the sustainable development of peoples everywhere. I will deal with the environmental aspects of the Earth Summit in the next chapter. Here I want to note how the UN summit jolted people into a new awareness of not just our common humanity wherever we live but also of the need to expand the very definition of the word "development."

The Earth Summit taught that a growth process benefitting only the wealthiest minority and maintaining or even increasing the disparities between and within countries is not development, it is exploitation. True development cannot be based on the North's culture of limitless economic growth. It encompasses the natural environment, social relations, education, production, fairer patterns of consumption, and well-being. It requires a recognition that the Earth's resources and capacity to sustain life are finite. It includes the passage from misery toward the possession of necessities, but it also means victory over social scourges, the growth of knowledge, and the acquisition of culture.

The UN shifted public thinking to a larger understanding that, while aid to the developing countries remained necessary, structural changes in the economic systems would prove far more important in reducing disparities. The UN Conference on Trade and Development, long arguing for better deals for the developing countries in trade and investment, succeeded in acquiring tariff concessions for the export of some manufactured products. The World Trade Organization, which manages trade negotiations around the world, has been able to lower import tariffs and agricultural subsidies to make it easier for developing countries to trade with the developed world in global markets. The new association of five emerging national economies called BRICS (Brazil, Russia, India, China, South Africa) has set up a $100 billion New Development Bank to fund projects in developing nations. These are among the structural changes in the world system that will reduce the Western-dominated control of the International Monetary Fund and the World Bank.

The international economic system is not yet negotiating the use of all the world's resources for the benefit of all (the vast mineral wealth at the bottom of the oceans beyond territorial limits is an example), but it has at least started to move in this direction. The old days of North–South distinctions are slowly giving way to the new idea of a global partnership to provide the human security that people everywhere crave, whether they live in shanties in Mumbai or condos in Manhattan.

THE NEW 2030 GOALS

A "global partnership for development" originated at the UN Millennium Summit in 2000. States created the Millennium Development Goals (MDGs), setting fifteen-year targets on aid, trade, debt relief, and improved access to essential medicine and new technologies. Civil society organizations, the private sector, philanthropic organizations, and international organizations were enlisted to expand government efforts to achieve eight goals. These included halving the rate of extreme poverty and hunger, universal primary education, the empowerment of women, reduced childhood mortality, improved maternal health, combating HIV/AIDS and other diseases, and environmental sustainability.

The target of reducing extreme poverty rates by half was met five years ahead of the 2015 deadline. Goals to increase water supplies and reduce the number of slums were also met. Those were striking accomplishments. However, we cannot ascribe total success to the MDGs. Some states made big improvements, others hardly any. Maternal health leaped forward, but most donor states did not meet official development assistance commitments. Zones of conflict wiped out economic gains. But overall, the MDGs, showing that the international community could be mobilized, drove the human development agenda forward at a faster pace than the world had ever seen. Putting the needs of people at the centre of the agenda and improving the collaboration between various sectors of society contributed to this accomplishment. Increasingly, development partnerships have replaced "handouts."

If confrontation on military matters still beclouds the UN's work, collaboration in the economic and social sphere has become a hallmark of the organization. Although the global partnership is more visible in responding to the effects of poverty than in attacking the roots of poverty, the first steps in implementing common responsibility for common security have been taken. A deeply interconnected global economy can no longer be managed only by its most successful players. The UN is truly responding to the demands of globalization.

Its success in mobilizing diverse sectors in addressing universal poverty has led the UN to attempt its most ambitious project yet. With the Millennium Development Goals set to expire in 2015, another plan was organized to take the development process to 2030. A team of thirty-two agency officials led by the UN Development Programme canvassed the views of thousands of people in eighty-eight countries and even opened a My World website in which more than five million people cast their votes on what they wanted for their lives. A clear message came through: people want good education, better health care and more job opportunities, and they want a sense of participation and inclusion in figuring out how to build their own future.

Secretary-General Ban led this process, which may well prove to be the hallmark of his administration. His document, "The Road to Dignity by 2030: Ending Poverty, Transforming All Lives and Protecting the Planet," reveals the scope of the new Sustainable Development Goals he has presented to world leaders.

To cope with an increasingly ageing, urbanized population expected to jump from the present seven billion to nine
billion by 2050, Ban wants no less than a universal agenda for a
shared future, one that is people-centred and planet-sensitive.
Humankind faces the same global challenges, he noted. Standards
based on the principles of human rights, the rule of law, equality,
and sustainability must be set to ensure the global common good.

"We now know that extreme poverty can be eradicated within one more generation," he said. "The MDGs have greatly contributed to this progress, and have taught us how governments,
business, and civil society can work together to achieve transformational breakthroughs." To synthesize the many goals and
targets into digestible form, Ban presented six themes for action:

Dignity: *to end poverty and fight inequalities.* No society
can reach its full potential without including the voices of
women, youth and minorities, indigenous people, the aged
and disabled, and migrants and refugees.

People: *to ensure healthy lives, knowledge, and the inclusion
of women and children.* Women must have access to health
and financial services and live in societies with zero tolerance
of violence against women and girls. The 1.8 billion youth
and adolescents today are a dynamic, informed, and globally
connected engine for change. Integrating their needs, rights,
and voices in the new agenda will be a key to success.

Prosperity: *to grow a strong, inclusive, and transformative
economy.* Innovation and investments in sustainable
infrastructure, settlement, industrialization, small and
medium enterprises, energy, and technology can generate

employment without harming the environment. A properly regulated, responsible, and profitable private sector is critical for employment, living wages, growth, and revenues for public programs.

Planet: *to protect our ecosystems for all societies and our children.* A development agenda must address climate change, halt biodiversity loss, and address desertification and unsustainable land use. Sustainable management of forests, marine ecosystems, and the atmosphere is necessary.

Justice: *to promote safe and peaceful societies, and strong institutions.* Access to fair justice systems, accountable institutions of democratic governance, measures to combat corruption and curb illicit financial flows, and safeguards to protect personal security are integral to sustainable development. More attention must be paid to rebuilding fragile societies after crises and conflicts. Reconciliation, peacebuilding, and state-building are critical for countries to overcome fragility and develop cohesive societies and strong institutions.

Partnership: *to catalyze global solidarity for sustainable development.* The sustainable development goals provide a platform for aligning private action and public policies. Transformative partnerships are built upon principles and values, a shared vision, and shared goals: placing people and planet at the centre of the agenda.

The strength of the agenda lies in the interweaving of its dimensions and its insistence that development goes far beyond the gross national product, and must include social progress, human well-being, justice, security, equality, and sustainability. Ban wants urgent action "to mobilize, redirect, and unlock the transformative power of trillions of dollars of private resources to deliver on sustainable development objectives." Casting an eye to the future, he said, "We have only scratched the surface of ethics-driven investment by the private sector."

Is all this too much for government and business leaders to swallow, let alone pay for? Perhaps. But the genius of the plan is to engage the private sector to invest in human development in the knowledge that governments will maintain political stability on the ground. Can massive human-centred economic and social development prove a bigger bulwark than constant militarism against the extremists and terrorists of the future? Will governments and corporate leaders as well as civil society activists have the vision and courage to pay the price of peace?

As Ban warns, the price of failure will be even higher than the multiple billions of dollars the Sustainable Development Goals will cost: "If the global community does not exercise national and international leadership in the service of our peoples, we risk further fragmentation, impunity and strife, endangering both the planet itself as well as a future of peace, sustainable development and respect of human rights."

The UN is investing a lot of its political capital in the Sustainable Development Goals. The audacity of assembling such a campaign to address the common security of all on the planet should be hailed as a leap forward in defining social justice in the modern world. If, in 2030, the campaign is judged successful, the UN may well be recognized for launching the transformation of the world from a culture of war to a culture of peace.

Ban and his successors will need continued dexterity to make the major leaders see that it is in their interests to use the resources of the world in an equitable way. Global stability is a bedrock of peace. Ban cannot confront governments and business, let alone issue any commands. He has no taxing power. He has to overcome the cynics and an indifferent media. He can only hold out a carrot and find ingenious ways of luring the national governments to bite. To succeed, the 2030 agenda must triumph over the old thinking that has for so long funded the gluttons of war while keeping peace on a starvation diet.

CHAPTER FOUR
CLIMATE CHANGE: A CHOICE FOR HUMANITY

The one issue that best illustrates how the work of the United Nations affects every individual on the planet is the environment. The Charter does not even mention the word "environment," yet the organization's preoccupation with a multitude of issues dealing with water, air, pollution, and global warming shows how the UN has evolved over the years to respond to the evolving needs of humanity. "Climate change," said Secretary-General Ban, "is the defining issue of our time."

The most visible part of the UN's work on the environment is the massive effort now underway to hold the rise in average global temperature to no more than two degrees Celsius above pre-industrial levels. Stopping, or at least containing, global warming by reducing the emission of greenhouse gases has become a rallying cry around the world. After prolonged prodding by the UN, governments in both the North and South agree that they have a shared responsibility to protect the climate by reducing carbon emissions. But getting commitments on binding targets in accordance with the different abilities of the rich and poor countries is a lot tougher.

The warming of the planet, which if continued will make life in many areas unsustainable, is palpable. In five reports starting in 1990, the UN Intergovernmental Panel on Climate Change has found that human-induced atmospheric concentrations of carbon dioxide, methane, and nitrous oxide have increased to levels unprecedented in at least the last 800,000 years. Global warming is already producing extreme weather patterns, reducing crop yields, worsening water shortages in arid areas, melting glaciers, and flooding low-lying lands. It's now a threat to human security in many places.

Many people think that because technology created this problem, technology can solve it. But pinpointing carbon reduction levels is only the start of setting humanity on a course of sustainable development. The underlying issue is our responsibilities as human beings interacting with one another on a planet where all the financial, energy, and trading systems are merging. Climate change is not only an overarching problem, it cuts to the core issue of building a world community based on rules protecting the common good. It forces us to think not only about the quality of life but also the primary issue of survival on the planet.

The rising temperature of the planet is a signal of the human distress of its inhabitants. Holding down the rise must be done immediately, but the sickness requires a holistic remedy, which almost by definition requires long-term work. Cooperation must replace competition to provide balanced development. That is what the UN has discovered and, through its forty specialized agencies and programs, is trying to implement.

Improving local weather forecasts, diminishing deadly air pollution, minimizing risk from disasters, managing and conserving forests, cutting emissions from vehicles, and making urban areas more energy efficient all contribute to a safer environment.

These steps, important in their own right, are also helping humanity to grasp the larger picture of what is at stake: can the expected nine billion people on Earth in 2050 live in a reasonably harmonious way, or will humans, plundering resources and despoiling the atmosphere, be reduced to their primal instincts of survival of the fittest?

TWO POINTS OF VIEW

In 1972, the UN first brought growing environmental problems to world attention with a global conference held at Stockholm. The divided views on responsibilities burst out into the open. Industrialized countries expressed their concern with pollution, conservation of genetic and natural resources, and the pressures on resources created by growing populations. Developing countries tended to dismiss environmental concern as the business of rich countries. Their energy and resource consumption were not high; industrial pollution was localized, if at all present. What concerned them was poverty and its effects: short life expectancies, infectious diseases, inadequate shelter, water, and sanitation. Reconciliation of opposite views began with the creation of the UN Environment Programme to stimulate a coordinated assessment of environment problems in both North and South and launch a number of initiatives to protect the oceans and the ozone layer.

As concern mounted over the global environment, the UN established a World Commission on Environment and Development, headed by Prime Minister Gro Harlem Brundtland of Norway. The report, "Our Common Future," issued a global call for strategies to promote economic and social development without further degradation of the environment. Brundtland coined the term "sustainable development." The integration of development and environment issues to improve human security was starting to be understood just at the moment when the concept of common security on East–West issues put a spotlight on arms reductions. The Cold War abruptly ended and a new vista of peace and prosperity loomed.

World attention on building a better world crested in 1992 with the UN's Earth Summit, a huge gathering of 178 states and thousands of representatives from non-governmental organizations, who came to Rio de Janeiro to lay the foundation for a global partnership between developing and industrialized countries based on mutual need and common interests. Maurice Strong, the visionary Canadian who had been secretary-general of the Stockholm conference, led the Rio meeting and told the assembly that growth models, which gave so much to the rich and so little to the poor, were not sustainable: "To continue along this pathway could lead to the end of our civilization." The conference was upbeat and the Rio Declaration established a primary principle: "Human beings are at the centre of concerns for sustainable development. They are entitled to a healthy and productive life in harmony with nature."

The Earth Summit produced international agreements on biodiversity, global warming, and forest principles, all of which broke new ground. The Biodiversity Convention is a legally binding treaty requiring inventories of plants and wildlife and plans to protect endangered species. The Framework Convention on Climate Change, also legally binding, commits signers to curb greenhouse gas emissions, but without a specific timeframe. The non-binding statement on Forest Principles sets goals for the protection of rainforests, although these were weakened by divided opinion: the North saw rainforests as a treasure trove of biodiversity and greenhouse gas sinks that absorb carbon dioxide, but some countries in the South insisted they were potential farmland and a free source of fuel.

The central document, *Agenda 21*, a detailed blueprint of 115 programs to deal with a host of environmental, economic, and social needs, was costed at $625 billion. But the industrialized countries balked at pledging their requested share of $125 billion. Their financial commitments did not extend much beyond existing aid programs. A moment for the world to make a giant leap forward was lost.

Measured in terms of timetables and money to implement programs, the Earth Summit could not be called very successful, though it certainly was not a failure. Its strength lay in the new understanding of the need for planetary management. The fusion of national political leaders, the demands of highly informed observers, and the impact of the media attention all widened decision-making about planet-wide development. In so doing, the Earth Summit defined how a new participatory world order should look.

"UNDENIABLE GLOBAL MOVEMENT FOR CHANGE"

Twenty years later, in 2012, the UN organized a Rio+20 conference, which broke all records for attendance. In addition to 192 governments, 50,000 people participated in 3,000 official Rio+20 events, many of them protesting exploitation of the earth's resources and the violation of the rights of indigenous peoples. Although Rio+20 succeeded in linking health issues to sustainable development and setting up the machinery to launch the 2015–2030 Sustainable Development Goals, the outcome of the conference was generally considered flat — at least, considering the scale of the problems. Ban took the long view, stating that Rio+20 was "further evolution of an undeniable global movement for change."

Governments have become adept at issuing global declarations whose lofty language obscures the lack of detailed financial commitments commensurate with the challenges. Putting cash on the line still scares governments, as if voters would revolt at higher taxes to fund sustainable development programs with long-range goals. Doubtless, a segment of the electorate would resist, but this element could be overcome by a combination of courageous leaders and education programs showing how stability of the planet and its people is in everyone's interests.

Thus the UN keeps charting new terrain in the human journey. Its accomplishments in expanding our thinking about what a "global neighbourhood" means are many and varied. The Law of the Sea Treaty, which entered into force in 1994 after many years of negotiation, provides a legal framework and institutions for managing and preserving the marine environment on a scale never before attempted. The big states are still resisting appropriating portions of the mineral wealth at the bottom of the oceans to landlocked states (usually the poorest of the world), but the principles of the global commons have been set.

In another realm of common heritage, the Outer Space Treaty, which entered into force in 1967, prohibits nations from placing weapons of mass destruction in space or on the moon or any other celestial body. The treaty also states that the exploration of space shall be carried out for the benefit of all countries. The peaceful use of space, however, still seems jeopardized by the major powers' present inability to conclude a treaty banning conventional arms from being stationed in space. UN leaders have good reason to be nervous that their campaign to prevent an arms race in outer space may founder.

THE PROMISE OF RENEWABLE ENERGY

Though the UN operates on several environmental fronts at the same time, the focus of its efforts must be on starting an actual decline in global emissions in the next decade and continuing the decline until there are no new emissions in the second half of the century. A UN conference in Copenhagen in 2009 to get such an agreement was derailed when governments could not summon up the political will to make time-bound commitments.

Since then, the United States and China, the world's two biggest emitters, entered into a bilateral deal in which the United States will double the speed of its current pollution reduction trajectory and China's emissions will peak in 2030 and then be reduced by a surge in nuclear power plants, wind farms, hydro-electric dams, and solar power. The US–China action has raised hopes that all nations will sign binding emission-reduction targets at a global conference in Paris in 2015. But moving many nations away from reliance on fossil fuels and towards low-carbon, resource-efficient economies will require enormous political will.

To stimulate development of a sustainable post-carbon future, in 2009 the UN created the International Renewable Energy Agency, which promotes the adoption of renewable energy, including bioenergy, geothermal, hydropower, ocean, solar, and wind energy. Although the agency stays out of the limelight, its research shows that doubling the world's share of renewable energy by 2030, from about 18 per cent in 2010 to 36 per cent, would help avoid the worst effects of climate change and would be cheaper than not doing so. In fact, said the agency's director, Adnan Z. Amin, when considering factors like the cost of ill health and environmental damage due to pollution, switching to renewable energy could save up to $740 billion per year by 2030: "If these costs were factored into energy prices, renewable energy and energy efficiency measures would be cheaper than fossil fuel alternatives." National governments are starting to move in this direction. Peru plans to generate 60 per cent of its electricity from renewable sources by 2024; Chile doubled its total renewable power capacity in 2014; Germany and Sweden will be carbon-free by 2050.

Nuclear power, a highly controversial form of alternate energy because of the radiation hazards involved, is treated by the United Nations as a hot potato. The very purpose of the International Atomic Energy Agency is to promote the safe, secure, and peaceful use of nuclear technologies. But the newer agency dealing exclusively with renewable energy will not support nuclear power as an alternative source of energy because of the high risks, the 2011 Fukushima disaster being the latest example. Article IV of the Non-Proliferation Treaty says states have an "inalienable right . . . to develop research, production and use of nuclear energy for peaceful purposes." The developing countries are not likely to yield that right, which they have seen as a gateway to catching up industrially to the Western countries. As in so many instances, the UN leadership ducks a head-on collision with nuclear proponents and quietly tries to find a new route to better security. In this case, better security means safe and affordable clean energy for a ravenous planet.

At one time, it was thought that nuclear power would be the energy wave of the future. But no longer. Were it not for government subsidies, nuclear power could not survive on private investment. Also, it cannot be denied that the development of nuclear energy is the first step to making a nuclear bomb. Nuclear power has far too many problems to be an attractive alternative to fossil fuels.

The most promising route to cooling down the planet is to negotiate binding commitments to reduce carbon emissions backed up by a massive campaign to invest in solar, wind, and other forms of renewable energy. This is exactly what the UN is promoting.

Inserting the methods to control climate change into the Sustainable Development Goals lifts up the debate over global warming to focus on the paramount issue: human security. The challenge of climate change is not just economic and political, it is fundamentally an ethical call to a more equitable use of the world's resources. It is more than caring for the well-being of the Earth, important as that is. It is caring for people, especially those deprived of elementary social justice by the voraciousness of the rich and powerful.

Climate change urgently reveals the choice humanity must now make: to selfishly pursue the benefits of the Earth, as the rich and powerful have done for so long, or to share resources more equitably for the common good. The UN is nudging the world toward sustainable development, and that may turn out to be its most lasting accomplishment.

CHAPTER FIVE
HUMAN RIGHTS: THE IMPOSSIBLE DREAM

When the United Nations adopted the Universal Declaration of Human Rights in 1948, it was hailed as a Magna Carta for humanity, a document rich in its affirmation that "all human beings are born free and equal in dignity and rights." How surprising that implementing this uplifting act of human unity has turned out to be so divisive. Or perhaps it isn't so surprising considering that the United Nations has always had to deal with a divided world.

In 2014, at one of its periodic debates on the state of the world, the Human Rights Council was the scene of a melee of charges and counter-charges. Italy, speaking for the European Union, rapped Russia for clamping down on civil society, China for arresting human rights defenders, and Israel for confiscating Palestinian lands. Russia complained about the rise of neo-Nazi groups in Ukraine. The United States said the problems in eastern Ukraine were caused by Russia's disregard for human rights in that region. France called on the international community to mobilize to end the savagery and atrocities of ISIL in Iraq, where more than two million Iraqis had fled the violence. Israel pointed to the responsibility of the Arab countries to address the misery, suffering, and despair caused by upheavals in those countries. The United Kingdom expressed strong concern about human rights violations in North Korea, Sudan, and South Sudan. Cuba said the United States held the record for abduction, torture, and racist implementation of the death penalty. Ecuador cited United States drone strikes as human rights violations.

It was not a friendly meeting.

The disputatious charges and counter-charges of governments have long characterized the UN's work in the human rights field. Even the original UN Commission on Human Rights had to be abandoned when Secretary-General Annan said it had become a place where states sought membership "not to strengthen human rights but to protect themselves against criticism or to criticize others." In its place, the General Assembly in 2006 created the Human Rights Council (HRC) where the forty-seven members are elected for fixed terms. Under the new system, every government is held accountable through the council's new universal review process.

Although, like its predecessor, the HRC is still sometimes charged with double standards and a preoccupation with investigating Israel, the new body has generally established a better track record of ferreting out human rights abuses and getting the Security Council to act. The HRC's international investigations of Libya, Côte d'Ivoire, Syria, Iran, and Belarus helped, to some extent, to alleviate crises in those areas by holding governments accountable. But it has been unable to do much to protect human rights in Afghanistan, Guantanamo Bay, Iran, Sri Lanka, Uzbekistan, and Zimbabwe.

When it overcomes political disputes, the Human Rights Council can become effective in raising norms for the treatment of people in distress. In different regions of the world, the council has mobilized governments to address the trafficking of women and children, internally displaced persons, involuntary disappearances, sexual orientation and gender identity, human rights of the disabled, the rights of persons before the law, and good governance in the promotion and protection of human rights.

Though the Human Rights Council has an undoubted value as a sort of watchdog on human rights, it rarely receives the plaudits of the more popular UN agencies, such as UNICEF and the UN Development Programme. Those agencies are action-oriented and the results in improved lives are readily apparent. But the HRC operates in the pit of ideological and racial prejudices. It is the place where hostilities, active or dormant, find an easy outlet. An accusatory environment does not usually produce hearty goodwill. Nonetheless, in recent years, the council seems to have found its footing as a watchdog for human rights violations. Its monitoring and reporting capacities have steadily increased. Injustices against human beings that in the past were kept in the shadows are today exposed to scrutiny and condemnation. It is unfair to blame the council for continued violations of human rights when governments, often with blatant hypocrisy, ignore commitments to the UN Charter and persecute their own people.

The Human Rights Council would not be nearly as effective as it is without the prodding of two outstanding non-governmental organizations, Amnesty International and Human Rights Watch. Founded in 1961 and now with seven million members, Amnesty International mobilizes public opinion to put pressure on governments to comply with international human rights and humanitarian law. Human Rights Watch, also an independent body set up initially to monitor compliance with the 1974 Helsinki Accords, investigates and exposes human rights abuses. Both are fearless in "naming and shaming" governments.

WHAT THE UNIVERSAL DECLARATION SET IN MOTION

Given the continued ideological divisions in the world that were by no means buried with the end of the Cold War, it is remarkable that the UN has achieved so much progress in advancing human rights. Much of this work has devolved from the expansion of the Universal Declaration of Human Rights into two covenants, one on civil and political rights, the other on economic, social, and cultural rights. Both set universal standards. Dozens of legally binding agreements on political, civil, economic, social, and cultural rights have followed through the years, building on the various parts of the original Universal Declaration. For example, the right not to be subject to arbitrary arrest, torture, and death is now codified. Freedom of religion is guaranteed. People can now claim a right to development.

By prosecuting and convicting war criminals, the UN tribunals, established after conflicts in the former Yugoslavia and Rwanda, helped to expand international humanitarian and international criminal law dealing with genocide and other violations of international law. Both tribunals have contributed to restoring peace and justice in the affected countries and in the region. Some 560 multilateral treaties — on human rights, terrorism, global crime, refugees, disarmament, trade, commodities, the oceans, and other matters — have been negotiated and concluded through UN work. Though the International Criminal Court, set up in 1998 to end impunity for perpetrators of war crimes, is an independent body, its origins lie in UN work. However, its effectiveness is weakened by the P5 and other powerful governments, who work behind the scenes to shield themselves and other nations they favour from the court's attention.

The fifteen-judge International Court of Justice, established by the Charter, operates in The Hague. The Court's role is to settle, in accordance with international law, legal disputes submitted to it by states and to give advisory opinions on legal questions referred to it by authorized United Nations organs. Unfortunately, the court does not have mandatory jurisdiction. Disputant states must agree beforehand to be bound to its decisions. Its most famous advisory opinion was the 1996 finding that the use of nuclear weapons would generally contravene humanitarian law and that states have an obligation to conclude negotiations for the elimination of nuclear weapons. This gave a shot in the arm to the nuclear disarmament movement, but the big powers were unmoved.

Even though the enforcement powers of international law are woefully weak, especially when compared with the stringencies of domestic laws, there is more protection for the life of every individual than in any previous period in history. Because the wide panoply of human rights has become etched in public discourse, it is extremely difficult today for governments to transgress international human rights law in secret. Social communications are a new weapon against tyrants.

The benefits of the expanding human rights agenda are not found everywhere, to be sure. There is still an immense amount of violence, deprivation, and suffering in the world, but the UN has raised global norms and created the political framework to make aspirations for a life free from violence and discrimination more real for billions of people through the years. To argue that the UN is ineffective because injustices jump out at us from the television screen makes as much sense as arguing that law is useless because a murder occurs in the local neighbourhood.

THE END OF COLONIALISM

It is not just individual rights that the United Nations protects. Entire peoples owe their freedom to the UN's decolonization work. When the organization was founded, nearly a third of the world's population lived in territories controlled by colonial powers. The General Assembly became a forum for freedom, and the legitimacy of continued "trusteeships" began to wane. In 1960, the UN adopted its landmark Declaration on the Granting of Independence to Colonial Countries and Peoples, affirming the right of all people to self-determination and calling for the speedy and unconditional end to colonialism. In all, eighty former colonies are now independent members of the UN. A special committee continues to monitor the situation in the remaining sixteen non-self-governing territories, which contain only two million people.

The ending of South Africa's notorious system of apartheid was undoubtedly one of the UN's greatest victories. Although South Africa was one of the original fifty-one signatories of the Charter, the segregationist society was never an easy fit with the UN's premise that all people are equal. Almost from the start, the General Assembly declared that apartheid was unacceptable racial segregation. It took a massacre in Sharpeville in 1960, where South African police opened fire on a crowd peacefully demonstrating against the hated pass laws, before the Security Council acted. An arms embargo, oil sanctions, and sports boycotts followed, and South Africa was suspended from the UN in 1974.

By this time, Nelson Mandela, one of the liberation leaders of the African National Congress, was serving a life sentence in prison for his human rights protests, and became the face of the anti-apartheid movement. He was released in 1990 and was elected the country's first black president four years later. When he addressed the General Assembly, President Mandela thanked the UN profusely: "We stand here today to salute the United Nations Organization and its member states, both singly and collectively, for joining forces with the masses of our people in a common struggle that has brought about our emancipation and pushed back the frontiers of racism."

MILESTONE FOR HUMANITY

With decolonization virtually complete, the UN turned its attention to building democracies as the most effective political environment for the realization of human rights. The Charter foresaw a rise in democratic values by stating, "the will of the people shall be the basis of the authority of government." It took time to develop, but now fostering democracy has become a cross-cutting issue in UN work, including peacekeeping, development, mediation, legal assistance in drafting constitutions, and election monitoring to strengthen fledgling democracies. Over the past two decades, the UN has provided electoral assistance to more than 100 countries — including logistics, civic education, and computer applications.

Cambodia, El Salvador, South Africa, Mozambique, Timor-Leste, Afghanistan, Burundi, the Democratic Republic of the Congo, Iraq, and Ukraine are just a few of the countries where the UN has sent teams to monitor elections.

World leaders pledged that the Millennium Development Goals would make the promotion of democracy, human rights, and freedoms a constant priority. Annan established a UN Democracy Fund for governments to contribute voluntarily to civic projects, mostly run by non-governmental organizations, to boost community development and the rule of law.

The value of the UN can and should be measured by its record on extending human rights to every region of the world. The way each of us lives depends on our ability to exercise our inherent dignity that comes with the gift of birth. Before the UN, human rights, to the extent they were understood at all, depended on wealth and power. Slavery was but the extreme manifestation of the cruelty with which humans treated one another. As the seventeenth-century English philosopher Thomas Hobbes said, life was "nasty, brutish, and short."

The ideas of freedom started to come alive during the American, French, and Russian revolutions, but it was only during the twentieth century that emancipation — equal status of individuals before the law — started to take hold. In Gandhi's resistance to tyranny through mass non-violent civil disobedience, we see the first modern assertion of human rights. Because the claims of human dignity cannot be confined to any one race or region, they need an institutional expression and, indeed, an institutional guarantor. The United Nations provides the global institutional expression even if it cannot yet be a complete guarantor.

The inauguration of the UN seventy years ago set in motion the development of the human rights agenda. That was certainly a major milestone for humanity. But the maturation of humanity has not yet reached a point where there is enforcement to protect the rights that have been delineated. If there were enforcement, we wouldn't have dire poverty or wars today. Global governance is still weak. Nonetheless, the condition of humanity as a whole has been elevated by the UN's constant emphasis on ever-widening application of human rights.

THE RIGHT TO PEACE

An effort is under way at the Human Rights Council to adopt a declaration stating that all individuals have the right to live in peace so they can fully develop all their capacities — physical, intellectual, moral, and spiritual — without being the target of violence. The end result of such thinking could well be the outlawing of war. While this would move humanity to a higher state of existence, the idea is not welcomed by those who are convinced that peace comes only through the flexing of military muscle. Arms-makers definitely reject the thought.

While codification of the right to peace is encountering obstacles, there is growing acceptance of the concept of a culture of peace, centring on the ethic of non-violence. The movement to a culture of peace, however "soft" it may appear compared to the "hard" decisions of warfare, offers hope for a future of peace.

The momentum of history, buttressed by new life-enhancing technologies, is on the side of the culture of peace. But can we — at least at this moment in history — turn the culture of peace into the right to peace? Does it follow that, because all human rights are universal, indivisible, interrelated, interdependent, and mutually reinforcing, all people are entitled to the right to peace in order to enjoy their inherent human rights? That is the issue the UN has put on the global agenda. Looking at the daily news, the right to peace does seem a very far reach. But it wasn't so long ago that the concept of a Universal Declaration of Human Rights would have been dismissed as an impossible dream.

CHAPTER SIX
WOMEN: THE POWER OF A NUMBER

Around the United Nations, the numeral "1325" possesses a lustre, like a star in the heavens that shines and inspires those who fall under its spell. Few UN resolutions are remembered just by their number and fewer still are embraced with a continuing passion. Security Council Resolution 1325 lives on, fifteen years after its adoption in 2000, inspiring women around the world to be a significant part of the peace process. Resolution 1325 is a perfect example of what the UN is all about: challenging the discriminations against half of humanity, holding up a vision of social justice, recognizing the obstacles that block progress, and renewing determination to overcome failures in moving humanity forward.

The year 2000 was perhaps a peak in post–Cold War hopefulness that the old animosities, which had so often had led to wars, could be put behind us. The United Nations proclaimed 2000 the International Year for the Culture of Peace. An International Decade for Peace was to follow. The terrorist attack on 9/11 was still in the future. In October 2000, the Security Council was chaired by Bangladeshi Ambassador Anwarul Chowdhury, who used this opportunity to bring global attention to what he called "the unrecognized, underutilized and under-valued contribution women have been making to preventing war, to building peace and to engaging individuals and societies to live in harmony."

Chowdhury had to overcome the initial opposition of the five permanent members of the council, but, in the end, his efforts produced a unanimous resolution — 1325. It recognized the inordinate impact of war on women, particularly through sexual- and gender-based violence, and the role that women should play in conflict management and building sustainable peace. Chowdhury maintained that it is not enough to insist that women are especially victimized by war but that women themselves need to be at the peace tables, involved in the decision-making and in peacekeeping teams. As he put it: "The main question is not to make war safe for women, but to structure peace in a way that there is no recurrence of war and conflict."

The need to protect women and girls from violence jumps out in the news every day. According to a 2013 global review of available data, 35 per cent of women worldwide have experienced either physical and/or sexual partner violence or non-partner sexual violence. Rape and female genital mutilation are still endemic in some places. Trafficking ensnares millions of women and girls in modern-day slavery. Women and girls represent 55 per cent of the estimated 20.9 million victims of forced labour worldwide.

Sexual violence in armed conflict is one of the most serious forms of violation or abuse of international humanitarian law and international human rights law. Increasingly, in Iraq, northern Nigeria, Syria, Somalia, and Mali (to name only a few places), violent extremists are taking control of territory, and directly threatening and targeting women, girls, and their communities. Between 2013–2014, the number of women and girl refugees skyrocketed. During and after conflict, more women die during childbirth, and more girls are forcibly married or sold as slaves. Fewer women work and participate in the economy, and fewer girls go to school. Human rights defenders are threatened and killed for speaking out against abuse. Journalists are silenced by violence and death. Teachers, students, and service providers are targeted.

SEXUAL CRIMES INVESTIGATOR

Violence against women in armed conflict stands out as the most egregious violation of women's human rights. In follow-up resolutions, the Security Council made sexual violence in conflict a war crime, demanding that parties to armed conflict take appropriate measures to protect civilians from sexual violence, including training troops and enforcing disciplinary measures. It also established a Special Representative for Sexual Violence in Conflict with a mandate to strengthen criminal accountability for rape and other sexual crimes in priority countries.

In 2012, Zainab Hawa Bangura, former Minister of Health in Sierra Leone, was appointed Special Representative for Sexual Violence in Conflict. Bangura has long been a social activist, speaking out against atrocities committed in Sierra Leone's civil war, and organizing a women's rights group, which campaigned for democratic elections. She later became foreign minister.

Bangura has used her post to increase the pressure on the Security Council for tougher measures to ensure that perpetrators of sexual violence against women are treated as war criminals. She produced a series of devastating reports on a number of countries. Investigating Bosnia and Herzegovina, she discovered a lack of services for 20,000 survivors of sexual violence crimes committed during the 1992–1995 conflict, with many survivors reluctant to come forward for fear of being stigmatized. Many of the alleged perpetrators had gained a form of impunity as policemen and politicians. Of the two hundred criminal cases laid, only twenty-nine led to sentencing.

In the Central African Republic, Bangura's team found that sexual violence was not marginal but rather central to the fighting, with rape common during house-to-house searches. Female politicians and female relatives of public officials were raped, kidnapped, and sometimes tortured. There were credible reports of girls being kept in military camps and becoming pregnant as a result of sexual slavery. Survivors were deterred from reporting because of the continuing presence of alleged perpetrators in the communities and the lack of a functional justice system. Bangura urged that peacekeepers be trained to prevent and respond to conflict-related sexual violence, and that reparations be done systematically rather than haphazardly. In South Sudan, the civilian population has been terrorized by deliberate ethnic targeting and gang rapes, many of them committed by the Lord's Resistance Army, a band of militant extremists led by Joseph Kony, who is wanted by the International Criminal Court.

While the prosecution of criminal acts relative to the gross number of those acts may be limited, the chief value of Bangura's work has been the exposure of this criminality. The knowledge of systematic investigations of sexual violence in war-torn areas acts as a deterrent of sorts. And gradually, the subject of how to deal with sexual violence is moving into the main discussions of UN peacebuilding techniques. Through regional or national action plans, eighty countries have committed to the women and peace and security agenda.

In the fifteen years since the passage of Resolution 1325, Chowdhury, who went on to lead the UN's efforts to develop the Culture of Peace documents, has kept pressure on the Security

Council to do more to implement the resolution as a "common heritage of humanity." He rejoiced when the Nobel Peace Prize committee, in awarding the prize in 2011 to three African women, cited Resolution 1325 for putting women on an equal footing with men in peace work.

Despite a slow start, women's participation and representation in conflict resolution and peace processes, a key feature of 1325, have improved. Of the eleven negotiations co-led by the UN in 2013, eight included at least one senior woman among negotiating delegates. The percentage of peace agreements committing to the improvement of the security and status of women and girls doubled in the 2011–2013 period. In 2014, the UN appointed Major General Kristin Lund of Norway as the first female commander of a UN peacekeeping force. The Security Council itself, long a male bastion, in 2014 had six female ambassadors (from Argentina, Jordan, Lithuania, Luxembourg, Nigeria, and the United States).

"The gains are remarkable," said Phumzile Mlambo-Ngcuka, former deputy president of South Africa, who heads UN Women. "However, it still leaves us with nearly half of all peace agreements that say nothing about women's rights or needs, and a majority of peace processes where women's minimal presence is an afterthought . . . Key decisions are still being made behind closed doors, deaf to the voices of those directly affected."

To obtain full gender equity, the proponents of 1325 want the resolution to be absorbed into all UN processes, not implemented on a piecemeal basis. Mlambo-Ngcuka argues that empowered women and girls are the best hope for sustainable development following conflict. They are the best drivers of growth, the best hope for reconciliation, the best buffer against the radicalization of youth and the repetition of cycles of violence.

The transformation to a society of full equal rights and fair opportunities for women has clearly been given a big boost by the UN. The organization UN Women, a department staffed by two thousand employees around the world, is one of the many products of 1325. It forges partnerships with governments and civil society groups to develop better education, health, and job opportunities for women. An increasing number of women's groups are allied with this work. For example, the Nobel Women's Initiative, composed of women Nobel Peace Prize laureates, uses the prestige of their award to magnify the power and visibility of women working for peace, justice, and equality.

WOMEN'S RIGHTS ARE HUMAN RIGHTS

The UN's concentration on improving the lives of women did not start with Resolution 1325. Equality of rights for women is a basic UN principle, set out in the preamble to the Charter. In 1979, the General Assembly adopted a women's bill of rights in the form of the Convention on the Elimination of All Forms of Discrimination Against Women. There have been several UN conferences devoted to women's rights, notably a spectacular gathering in Beijing in 1995, which issued a strong platform calling for gender equity on many fronts. Also, the UN's activities have been only a part of the worldwide feminist movement, which has long campaigned for reforms on issues such as women's reproductive rights, domestic violence, maternity leave, equal pay, women's suffrage, sexual harassment, and sexual violence.

Previously, women's rights were seen as just that, a campaign to raise the status of women in the world. Their rights were frequently interwoven with children's rights. Resolution 1325, however, lifted women's rights beyond the concern of women to a mainline human rights issue. The distinct contribution of the

United Nations to women is to enlarge understanding that our society is not complete without the full participation of women, not just because they hold up half the sky, but because the integral and inherent nature of human rights draws no distinction between the sexes. If the UN stands for anything, it is for a holistic view of humanity. Men and women are now seen as equal partners in the continued development and preservation of the planet.

Of course, this lesson still has to be learned by many men in the UN system, who see women as appendages rather than main players. The cultural backgrounds of many UN officials and delegates account for these ongoing attitudes. However, misogyny, still a dominant characteristic in much of society today, has a harder time prevailing in the modern UN, where, increasingly, senior posts are held by competent women and the prospect of a woman secretary-general is very much on the horizon.

To break down some of the remaining barriers against women, the UN launched in 2014 the HeForShe campaign to get one billion men to support gender equality issues. The spokesperson for the campaign is UN Women Goodwill Ambassador Emma Watson, a British actor, who appealed to a UN audience to free men as well as women from gender stereotyping: "I want men to take up this mantle. So their daughters, sisters, and mothers can be free from prejudice but also so that their sons have permission to be vulnerable and human too — reclaim those parts of themselves they abandoned and in doing so be a more true and complete version of themselves." At the UN, feminism is for men too.

CHAPTER SEVEN
CIVIL SOCIETY: GIVING PEOPLE A VOICE

Votes at the United Nations are cast by governments, but the ideas behind the resolutions are mostly shaped by a vast network of non-governmental organizations (NGOs) playing roles ranging from intense activism to scholarly formulation of new concepts of human security.

The movement forward in the key areas of human security — arms control and disarmament, economic and social development, environmental protection, and human rights — has been inspired and pushed by huge numbers of individuals now collectively known as civil society. They can be found any day at the UN, observing formal meetings, lobbying government delegates, sometimes running their own seminars, publishing documents that break new ground and, in general, reminding governments that the UN Charter starts with the words, "We the peoples of the United Nations . . ."

The term "civil society" is so all-embracing that it can include virtually any group outside government itself, including those whose activities are far beyond UN interests. But at the UN, the term is generally used for non-profit organizations composed of humanitarian-minded individuals devoted to the improvement of the human security agenda.

In 2015, there were 4,165 such organizations with official consultative status at the Economic and Social Council. They even have their own organization, the Conference of NGOs, dedicated to strengthening the participation of NGOs in the decision-making processes. The UN Development Programme has a fifteen-person Civil Society Advisory Committee, which UNDP Administrator Helen Clark hailed as "a driving force extending post-2015 consultations and reaching new constituencies and a wider range of stakeholders." They frequently provide a valuable critique: the small German-based NGO, Global Policy Forum, publishes incisive monitoring of all UN activities.

Although Article 71 of the Charter made room for NGOs in UN debates and, in fact, many participated in the San Francisco founding conference of the UN, their status has always been controversial.

Some governments are decidedly cool to the idea of "unelected" people telling them what to do; other governments include NGOs on their delegations. NGOs are sometimes resented, and sometimes encouraged. Some NGOs want to work within the parameters of existing political systems in a cooperative manner, others oppose economic and social systems that they claim are the cause of problems and thus they campaign for systemic change. Some operate in think tanks, and others take to the streets. Some run their own programs, particularly in the aid field, while others monitor the implementation of legislation, notably in the human rights field. Some depend on government funding, or at least are careful not to jeopardize their charitable status and thus the official receipts their donors receive for tax deductions, while others shun government money.

There is no easy categorization of NGOs. The most general characterization is they advocate for change, constantly challenging the status quo.

Nor can a sharp line be drawn between official work and the free-floating spirit of NGOs. Government representatives and independent civil society experts regularly intersect on UN commissions whose reports prepare the way for UN policy development. Some former government officials have become leading NGO advocates and not a few NGO experts have entered government service.

Whether as insiders or outsiders, NGOs have made their presence felt. In 2012, 2,400 representatives of NGOs attended the government-led Earth Summit in Rio, many of them leading discussions at the parallel NGO-led Global Forum. In 1995, 4,000 accredited NGO representatives participated in the Beijing World Conference on Women. In 1982, one million people marched in New York for the abolition of nuclear weapons in an effort to spur on a special UN session on nuclear disarmament.

While the development of human security policy certainly cannot be ascribed solely to NGOs, they have had a profound influence in raising the public conscience and demanding a more serious government response to the distresses afflicting humanity. The Arms Trade Treaty, the Mine Ban Treaty, the Comprehensive Nuclear-Test-Ban Treaty, and the many UN treaties on human rights and agreements on climate change are just the start of a long list of UN legal instruments whose origins lie in the advocacy and involvement of civil society.

In some cases, a dynamic NGO can achieve impressive results when interacting with governments and the UN secretariat. One example is the Global Centre for the Responsibility to Protect, led by human rights activists who work with governments and foundations within the UN and regional settings to protect populations from mass atrocities. The International Crisis Group, Human Rights Watch, Oxfam International, Refugees International, and the World Federalist Movement–Institute for Global Policy — all highly respected NGOs — are also heavily involved in practical steps to implement the Responsibility to Protect doctrine, concentrating on several African and Middle Eastern countries. The executive director is Dr. Simon Adams, whose long experience as a human rights advocate in South Africa, Ireland, and Rwanda has given him knowledge few government officials can match.

The Intergovernmental Panel on Climate Change, established by the UN, owes its high standing to the impeccable work of the scientists around the world who participate. The nuclear disarmament field is crowded with civil society specialists whose forums at the UN are regularly attended by government delegates. Countless voluntary aid workers are on the front line in poverty areas helping the displaced, refugees, and other vulnerable people.

All this work is an immense contribution to the UN's goals in making the world a safer, more equitable place. Not every NGO is a perfect instrument of idealism and several are caught up in turf wars, but on the whole, civil society groups have given a more human, exciting dimension to the UN. They break barriers that constrain government and UN officials and show how humanity can truly be freed from the ravages of war and poverty.

DEVELOPING GLOBAL GOVERNANCE

Without any formal declarations as such, civil society at the UN is effectively contributing to new forms of world governance, reaching across diverse cultures and races and using the modern tools of social communication. True, national sovereignty still dominates political decisions. But governments are learning that national policies alone won't solve global problems. Cooperation for the common good is essential in the modern world. Many NGOs, with their vision and commitment to an equitable social order, have pushed governments to more human-centric policies.

NGOs' insistence on greater participation in decision-making processes is strengthening governance in the world. The UN has found that well-governed countries are less likely to be violent and less likely to be poor. Giving a voice to people in determining their own futures widens the governance process. It enhances such democratic values as equity, participation, pluralism, transparency, accountability, and the rule of law. These values translate into practical UN programs: election monitoring, building independent judiciaries, fighting corruption, and stabilizing pricing and banking systems. NGOs play critical roles in this wide governance canvas. It is no surprise that, precisely because civil society is so enmeshed in UN operations, the organization is such a trusted entity by global publics.

The UN calls this "multistakeholder governance," an unwieldy term (one of the UN's less attractive features is a proclivity for arcane language), which means that governments and civil society each play an active role in setting priorities to meet the needs of vulnerable people and a fragile Earth. Or to put it another way, when people are given a voice, their governments are more likely to invest in national policies that reduce weaponry, protect the environment, and lift the poor out of poverty. The UN rightly claims that good governance provides the setting for a fairer world for all.

But these aspirations need to be grounded in reality. The reality is that market forces drive governments, which generally means that the fittest do very well (under either capitalism or communism). The corporate agenda dominates discussions, whether the subject is nuclear weapons, trade and finance policies, or protection of the environment.

The UN has tried to inject a number of ethical principles into business by the formation of the Global Compact, an arrangement whereby businesses pledge adherence to internationally proclaimed human rights, particularly in labour and anti-corruption measures. With 12,000 corporate participants from 145 countries, the Global Compact is the largest voluntary corporate responsibility initiative in the world. Ban Ki-moon said it has helped generate a major shift in corporate mindset in just one decade: "Enlightened leaders are making sustainability a core part of business strategy."

Still, global governance needs a stronger basis than voluntary participation. No city council or legislature is run by volunteers. Many NGOs, convinced that the present emanations of global governance are ineffective and undemocratic, are seeking the installation of a legislative assembly into the UN. The Campaign for a United Nations Parliamentary Assembly, which would integrate parliamentarians from around the world into UN decision-making, is gathering support. The idea of citizens directly electing their own representatives to a world legislative body undoubtedly has some appeal, not least because such voting would conceivably counter the present UN system in which diplomats vote according to their governments' instructions. After all, Kofi Annan said, "The parliamentary voice — the voice of the people — must be an integral component of the work of the United Nations."

Article 22 of the Charter permits the General Assembly to establish subsidiary organs "as it deems necessary for the performance of its functions." With enough pressure to overcome the resistance of the major governments, which do not take kindly to the idea of power-sharing, a parliamentary wing is feasible. The most promising development to strengthen global governance in the near term would be the acceptance of the Inter-Parliamentary Union, a group of members of 166 parliaments, as a consultative assembly at the UN. The introduction of such voices into an institutionalized setting would at least be a step forward in bringing citizens' concerns into the world arena.

As for a world government to deal with all the problems of a globalized world, that too is the fervent wish of a number of NGOs dedicated to the reasonable idea of a single common political authority over all humanity. It hardly needs to be said that the UN is not, and was not designed to be, a world government, rather a forum for sovereign states to debate issues and determine collective courses of action. The World Federalist Movement, which goes back to the earliest days of the UN, promotes a global federalist system of strengthened and accountable global institutions. Who knows how the inhabitants of the world a hundred or two hundred years from now will decide what is in their best interests? For the foreseeable future, however, the best contribution to global governance is to urgently strengthen the UN's ability to get national governments to cooperate in building the conditions for peace. NGOs are good at that.

YOUTH: BIG DIVIDENDS AHEAD

The UN's concentration on youth portends an even stronger civil society participation in global decision-making in the future. The UN even has an Envoy on Youth, Ahmad Alhendawi of Jordan, who advocates for youth across the UN system. The 1.8 billion young people (defined as those between ages ten and twenty-four) constitute both a problem and an opportunity for the UN. Meeting the education and job needs of such a huge number is an overwhelming challenge for many governments; yet young people's intuitive understanding of globalization combined with their prowess using the tools of social communication may well strengthen global governance in years ahead.

Alhendawi, who visited twenty-four countries in 2014, says youth are an asset for the future and need investment today to open up opportunities for their vigorous participation in society. He wants youth involved at the UN's discussions on the great themes of climate change and sustainable development goals. "Democracies cannot be sustained without the participation of young people," he said. "Their involvement will pay big dividends in the future."

CHAPTER EIGHT
REFORMING THE UN: AN INJECTION OF CASH

Reform of the United Nations has been called for from the very start of the organization. It is a subject that never goes away.

Most of the time, the discussion centres around the power to veto Security Council resolutions possessed by the five permanent members. Get rid of the veto and we'll have world peace, say the reformers. That is a proposition unlikely to be tested in the foreseeable future because, from the very start, the P5 have jealously guarded this right they gave themselves at the UN's inauguration. Besides, since the P5 pay 40 per cent of the organization's bills, they feel justified in holding a commanding voice in its decisions.

Instead of bemoaning what cannot be changed easily, the international community should focus on such practical measures as enlargement of the Security Council so that its permanent membership (the United States, Russia, the United Kingdom, France, and China) would be more representative of the modern world, and on a more democratic method of selecting the secretary-general. Also, summit meetings of the Security Council are a rare event; they should be annual.

Important as these improvements would be, there is an even more urgent reform required — changing the major powers' attitudes toward prioritizing the UN when building the conditions for peace. The powerful states treat the UN as if it were something to be tolerated rather than championed. They frequently marginalize the UN in the peacemaking process instead of putting it front and centre. They deprive it of funding, criticize its bureaucracy, and undermine their own commitments made when they signed the Charter.

Hanging on to the outmoded prerogatives of sovereign states accustomed to fighting wars, the big players do not want a robust international institution to enforce peace. They have not accepted the reality that preventing conflict is a lot cheaper than waging war. Although they frequently join in admirable aspirations for peace, they do not put teeth into the implementation of international law, which the Security Council was created to enforce. They want to keep the UN in a subservient position. In short, the powerful states do not fully respect, and certainly lack confidence in, their own institution.

There is no greater indicator of this lack of confidence than the inadequate funding provided by governments. In 2015, countries paid $2.9 billion for the UN's regular budget (the New York City police department costs $4.8 billion annually). This bargain ranks with the greatest deals of all time, which includes the original purchase of Manhattan from American Indians for $16.

The assessed United States share is 22 per cent, a far greater percentage than any other country (China pays 5.1 per cent, Russia 2.4 per cent). The imbalance in the payment structure is astonishing. Dozens of countries, not only the poorest by any means, pay less than 1 per cent. Even India with its burgeoning economy pays only 0.666 per cent. A twenty-first-century overhaul of the payment system is essential, but whenever this subject arises, the United States, the host country, surprisingly declines to have its load significantly lightened on the grounds that its influence would subsequently lessen.

Peacekeeping costs an additional $8 billion per year, and this is also assessed to all members. Much of the humanitarian work of the UN is paid for by members' voluntary contributions. All told, the entire body of work of the UN, including peacekeeping and the sweeping economic and social development programs of forty specialized agencies and programs, costs $30 billion per year. This works out to about four dollars per person on the planet. It is only 1.76 per cent of the $1.7 trillion that nations spend annually on arms.

Many states think UN reform is a matter of streamlining the organization to produce "tangible measurable results," as if stripping UN programs to the bare bones would magnify results. That the UN managers have already brought in international public accounting standards, installed new procurement rules, and updated information technology systems, saving hundreds of millions of dollars a year, is swept aside by fatuous criticism.

It is hard to get governments to understand that investing in peace and sustainable development is in the common interests of all. This requires educating the public about what the UN does and this in turn requires sufficient resources. With a limited budget, the UN tries to put information about itself on its various websites. The Office of Disarmament Affairs publishes a daily digest of news and analysis of security matters unmatched in scope by any other source. Anyone who wants to be informed can readily access the basic facts. But there is a huge disconnect between the magnitude of the UN's agenda and the public understanding of the challenges. Appointing Daniel Craig, the latest film incarnation of James Bond, as a UN Global Advocate for the elimination of mines will undoubtedly draw the attention of many to UN work. "As 007, Mr. Craig had a 'licence to kill,'" Ban Ki-moon drily noted. "We are giving him a 'licence to save.'" The UN's public information department, however, can only do so much.

The leaders of governments should recognize their responsibilities to show in words and actions that they highly value the one world body that underpins common security. That is the first and most urgent reform needed by the United Nations.

ENLARGING SECURITY COUNCIL

It is hard to count the number of conferences, papers, and proposals dedicated to reform of the Security Council. One workable idea — the P5 voluntarily limiting the use of its veto, so that at least it would not be used to bar UN military action in mass atrocity situations — is only slowly gaining support. It is disgraceful that the major powers have prevented the UN from developing its own permanent peacekeeping force or even a standby force. Again we see how practical reforms at the UN are either undermined or blocked by myopia. Despite the evident need for the global enforcement of international law, militarily and judicially, the big powers are not yet ready to put the common good ahead of their selfish interests.

Leaving aside the disputatious question of the P5 veto power, there appears to be general agreement that the composition of the P5, which constitutes only 26 per cent of world population and is heavily weighted in the West, is not a fair representation of the modern world. But agreement stops there. States have been unable to come to a consensus on whether new permanent members should be added, or whether enlarging the number of rotating non-permanent members (presently ten) would be sufficient reform.

Many scenarios envision Brazil, India, Germany, and Japan, who have formed their own club for the purpose, being given permanent seats without veto power. But that would leave Africa unrepresented. Nigeria and South Africa, the two strongest contenders, are not willing to yield to the other. Should Europe get a third seat with Germany? Would the United Kingdom and France agree to be melded into one European seat? Would the Council be able to function with some permanent members having veto power and others not? Would it be better to forget about adding permanent members and just add more non-permanent members with longer terms than the present two years?

These questions have preoccupied the debates over the years — and nothing happens. Jealousies, distrust, and lethargy seep through the minutes of the meetings. When a good idea about power sharing surfaces, it is usually lost in a fog of interpretations. A power-sharing model, the Binding Triad would enable the General Assembly to pass binding resolutions by a supermajority vote based on three elements: a majority of members, those whose combined contributions in dues comprise a majority of the UN budget, and those whose populations form a majority of the world population.

Creative ideas to fund the UN, such as a global tax on currency transactions, a carbon tax, or a tax on the arms trade, have also fallen by the wayside. The UN needs a cash injection. Although at least half the members of the UN contribute only a pittance, they are often the biggest beneficiaries. UN reform should start with all countries, large and small, paying more.

OPEN ELECTION OF SECRETARY-GENERAL

One needed UN reform, which would not have "financial implications" (another favourite UN term), would have lasting impact. The selection of the secretary-general every five years has momentous consequences on which issues will be brought before the Security Council. Article 99 of the Charter permits the secretary-general to bring before the council any matter that in his or her opinion threatens international peace and security. The selection of a person with such power should be an open process. Instead, the Security Council operates as a closed shop, secretly vetting candidates and submitting one name to be voted on by the General Assembly. P5 members have blackballed candidates they did not like. Transparency and democracy go out the window.

To open up the process in time for the 2016 election of the successor to Ban Ki-moon, a new organization of NGOs, 1 for 7 Billion, is campaigning for the General Assembly to scrutinize candidates in open sessions with, of course, no veto by the P5. An experienced and able secretary-general can set the tone for international diplomacy, as well as helping the various parts of the UN system function more effectively. A more open and inclusive selection process would give future secretaries-general a stronger mandate to strengthen the UN's credibility, authority, and popular appeal.

How powerful will Washington, Moscow, Beijing, London, and Paris permit the UN to become? That is the key question underlying all the issues concerning UN reform.

CONCLUSION
FROM TERRORISM TO A CULTURE OF PEACE

The mélange of hopes, accomplishments, and problems of the United Nations is seen dramatically in the terrorism issue, which has the world on edge. It is not just a question of Islamist extremists establishing caliphates in the Middle East; every country is now vulnerable to local branches of Al-Qaeda and its offshoots. Where will terrorism strike next? Using the UN's broad programs of action is critical to defeating terrorism.

Terrorism is growing because states still resist the fundamental lesson the UN has taught for seventy years: war does not produce peace. The War on Terror, rashly proclaimed after 9/11, unleashed chaos in Afghanistan and Iraq and has led to the recruitment of thousands of terrorist fighters. It has been a failure of monumental proportions. The only effective way to counter world terrorism is by strengthening UN international partnerships to use all the political, economic, social, and legal instruments available — not by bombing.

Blocking the ability of terrorists to assemble, communicate, transfer money, and acquire arms has preoccupied the United

Nations for more than a decade. The four pillars of the UN's Global Counter-Terrorism Strategy — countering the appeal of terrorism, combating terrorism, strengthening the UN's ability to deal with terrorism, and protecting human rights in combating terrorism — contain within them the potential to end terrorism as a worldwide threat.

When the Security Council held a summit meeting in September 2014, chaired by US President Obama, it unanimously adopted a resolution aimed at suppressing the recruitment of foreign terrorist fighters. Resolution 2178 called on states to take steps to prevent suspected terrorists from entering or transiting their territories and to share information on criminal investigations, interdictions, and prosecutions. This resolution added to the fourteen universal legal instruments to prevent terrorist acts the UN started adopting in 1963. The organization stepped up its anti-terrorism work following 9/11. The landmark Security Council Resolution 1540 prevents weapons of mass destruction from falling into the hands of terrorists.

The UN teaches that extremism and violence are spawned by tyranny, inequalities, and bad governance. Few crises erupt without warning. They build up over years of human rights grievances and the denial of basic economic and social rights. Unfortunately, states are still reluctant to implement the UN's comprehensive response to terrorism. Every time a terrorist attack occurs, the first response of most governments is to call for military action. "Killing evil" becomes a mantra. Erratic political leadership panics with each new outbreak.

Those who want to uncover the reasons behind violence are accused of condoning terrorism. It is time to stop such knee-jerk, one-dimensional reactions. The outbreak of radical extremism reveals the deep disorder in the world, which can only be corrected by summoning up all the resources of humanity to develop procedures to protect the common good. That is what the United Nations does.

The response to terrorism may have to include military action, when authorized by an effectively functioning Security Council, but it must go far beyond that to ferret out injustices in the social order. Social, economic, and political exclusion are invariably the breeding grounds for terrorism.

Assisting young people to see that they can obtain a good future without violence requires the full force of economic and social programs that are still only marginally applied in areas of greatest potential conflict. Preventing the development of new bands of terrorists is more promising for humanity than dealing with barbarism when it breaks loose. Fostering interfaith cooperation raises hopes that violent religious extremism can be overcome.

Such long-range action should not be dismissed as inconsequential to the demands of the moment. Of course, existing terrorism must be met today by the rule of law. The UN upholds this. But the UN has the collective wisdom to know that the anger and alienation that produces terrorism must also be addressed. Good governance must operate on several fronts at once — policing, retribution, restoration, rehabilitation, and reconciliation. That is what the UN, in its fullness, provides.

The United Nations is the home of the Alliance of Civilizations, created in 2006 to counter the forces that fuel religious polarization and extremism, particularly between Muslims and the West. The Alliance speaks effectively against the radical extremists who pervert religion, in this case the teachings of Islam, for their own ends. By connecting governments, parliamentarians, local authorities, civil society, the media, and religious leaders, it is building trust and understanding between diverse communities.

Similarly, the United Nations Educational, Scientific and Cultural Organization (UNESCO) is dedicated to "building peace in the minds of men and women."

These UN bodies help us to understand that it is not enough just to fight terrorists. Terrorism challenges us to build a better society. As Secretary-General Ban puts it: "The most effective tool to combat terrorism is by working to achieve the United Nations core goals of strengthening peace and security, the promotion of human development and, above all, the observance of human rights and the rule of law." Even US Secretary of State John Kerry admitted: "Eliminating the terrorists that confront us today actually only solves part of the problem. We have to do more to avoid an endless cycle of violent extremism. We have to transform the very environment from which these forces emerge." Those words need to be applied to full support of UN programs.

A CULTURE OF PEACE

From the immediacy of coping with today's critical issues to the long-range betterment of the world for our grandchildren, the United Nations contributes to the well-being of humanity in ways that were hardly dreamed about a hundred years ago. That it has been able to uplift the whole of humanity in so many ways in its first seventy years is astounding. That it is still deprived of full political support and adequate funding is shameful. Perhaps that is the way of the world. We weave from majesty to oblivion.

The United Nations is by far the best instrument we have to cope with the common threats the world faces in the twenty-first century. When the Security Council acts in unity, it gets results: measures to curb the proliferation of nuclear weapons, elimination of Syria's chemical weapons, effective peacekeeping in the Central African Republic and other war-torn places. Global poverty, child mortality, and maternal deaths have been cut in half in the past twenty years by UN agencies.

Despite these accomplishments, the UN is too often dismissed by those in a hurry for instant solutions to problems that lie deep within the psyches of peoples and nations across the globe. The new instruments for peace the UN is trying to build are in the hands of fallible people, but that does not mean the essential ideas of justice the UN is promoting are deficient. On the contrary, it is the very largeness of the UN agenda that requires more time for fulfillment than those wedded to the daily news seem willing to allow. Those who do see the value of the UN ideal need to exercise courage and patience.

The UN should be regarded as a central dynamic organization helping populations everywhere to move forward. It is saving the peace in diverse regions and lifting millions out of destitution. It is trying to prevent nuclear warfare and environmental catastrophe. It is developing everyone's human rights. Its core message insists seven billion people can live together in a culture of peace and emphasizes non-violence as a starting point. It is the base of our hopes for lasting peace.

With all its limitations, the United Nations is the most successful world political body humanity has ever known. No other peace effort in history — including the Thirty Years' Peace between Athens and Sparta in 446 BC, the Peace of Westphalia of 1648, which set up the nation-state system, or the ill-fated League of Nations, established after World War I — has had such a penetrating effect on the human journey.

Now, unfolding a plan to take the world to 2030, the UN is advancing a universal agenda for sustainable development applying to all countries. This is the UN at its best. It has learned a lot about itself and the world in its first seventy years. Now it's time for the world to give the UN the support it needs for the next seventy.

There is no doubt the UN needs to find better ways to communicate this core message and why the organization needs stronger support. Also, government leaders should vigorously proclaim the values of the UN. But perhaps most of all, "we the peoples of the United Nations" need to take the message in our own hands. It is our human security the United Nations is trying to protect.

ACKNOWLEDGEMENTS

Thirty years ago, I wrote a book, *United Nations: Divided World*, to mark the fortieth anniversary of the organization and thanked a list of people who had helped me understand the accomplishments, problems, and potential of the UN. Since then, my involvement with the UN has deepened, especially since I became Canada's Ambassador for Disarmament to the UN and subsequently Chairman of the UN Disarmament Committee. It is impossible to thank all the diplomats, officials, and civil society activists who have, over the years, added to my understanding of the many sides of the UN.

I am indebted to former Secretary-General Javier Perez de Cuellar, who gave me a bound copy of the Charter in the UN's six official languages and taught me the patience required for multilateral diplomacy. Two former heads of the UN's disarmament office, Jayantha Dhanapala of Sri Lanka and Sergio Duarte of Brazil, and the current incumbent, Angela Kane of Germany, shared with me their deep insights into the UN machinery. Helen Clark, former Prime Minister of New Zealand and head of the UN Development Programme, contributed to my thinking about the vast agenda under the general heading of economic and social development. Maurice Strong, the indefatigable Canadian who pioneered the UN's environmental work, and two Canadian ambassadors to the UN, the late Saul Rae and the late George Ignatieff, were all mentors to me and enlarged my horizons to see the fullness of the UN.

In the current UN years, former Under-Secretary-General Anwarul Chowdhury, who has done so much to develop the concept of the culture of peace, has guided me steadily for many years. Randy Rydell, former senior policy adviser in the disarmament office, gave me the benefit of his extensive knowledge of the Organization. Maher Nasser, former Acting Head of the UN Communications and Public Information, Ramu Damodaran, Deputy Director, Outreach Division, and Ylva Braaten of the Dag Hammarskjöld Library all helped me in the preparation of this book. Jonathan Granoff, president of the Global Security Institute, made astute observations on the UN's great potential. Tariq Rauf, director, disarmament affairs at the Stockholm International Peace Research Institute, has helped me in nuclear disarmament issues for three decades.

Carolyn McAskie, former UN Assistant Secretary-General for Peacebuilding, shared with me her experiences in managing UN peace operations in politically complex and challenging conflicts. Bill Pace, executive director of the World Federalist Movement–Institute for Global Policy, gave me much background information on the Responsibility to Protect doctrine. Alistair Edgar, executive director of Academic Council on the United Nations System, provided valuable insights into civil society's interaction with the UN.

I want especially to thank Walter Dorn, professor at Canadian Forces College, for his comments and for allowing me, in Chapter One, to draw on his article, "Unsung Mediator: U Thant and the Cuban Missile Crisis," which describes in great detail the historic but underappreciated role former Secretary-General Thant played in ending the Cuban Missile Crisis.

Kate White, president and CEO of the United Nations Association in Canada, and Joan Broughton, her assistant, gave me much background information. Firdaus Kharas, former executive director of the United Nations Association in Canada, has long provided me with valuable insights into the UN. Elizabeth May, leader of the Green Party of Canada, provided a fresh perspective. John Trent, editor of *United Nations and Canada*; Peter Langille, senior research fellow at the Centre for Global Studies, University of Victoria; and Peggy Mason, president of the Rideau Institute on International Affairs, all broadened my understanding of the UN's peacemaking activities. Jim Creskey, publisher of *The Embassy* in Ottawa, always provides me with the encouragement I need.

My daughter Evita Roche gave me the original idea for this book. When I showed my publisher, Jim Lorimer, a rough outline, he instantly said he wanted it. I deeply appreciate his confidence in me, and I am grateful for the work of the Lorimer team, including Emma Renda, Nicole Habib, Kendra Martin, and Dan Campbell.

The manuscript was read by Fergus Watt, executive director of the World Federalist Movement–Canada; David Evans, former editorial page editor at the *Edmonton Journal*; and Ruth Bertelsen, who has guided me through many of my previous books. They provided corrections and improvements and I am deeply grateful to them. Any remaining errors are my responsibility.

As for so many years, I continue to be helped in my daily life by Khalid Yaqub, Edel Maran, and Bonnie Payne.

To all of the above, I express my affection and continuing gratitude.

Douglas Roche
Edmonton, March 2015

SELECTED BIBLIOGRAPHY

Annan, Kofi (with Nader Mousavizadeh). *Interventions: A Life in War and Peace*. New York: The Penguin Press, 2012.

Kennedy, Paul. *The Parliament of Man: The Past, Present and Future of the United Nations*. Toronto: HarperCollins, 2006.

Lipsey, Roger. *Hammarskjöld: A Life*. Ann Arbor: The University of Michigan Press, 2013.

Meisler, Stanley. *Kofi Annan: A Man of Peace in a World of War*. Hoboken, New Jersey: John Wiley & Sons Inc., 2007.

Meisler, Stanley. *United Nations: The First Fifty Years*. New York: The Atlantic Monthly Press, 1995.

Schechter, Michael G. *United Nations–sponsored World Conferences: Focus on Impact and Follow-up*. Tokyo: United Nations University Press, 2001.

Schlesinger, Stephen C. *Act of Creation: The Founding of the United Nations*. Boulder, Colorado: Westview Press, 2003.

Traub, James. *The Best Intentions: Kofi Annan and the UN in the Era of American World Power*. New York: Farrar, Straus and Giroux, 2006.

Weiss, Thomas G. and Ramesh Thakur. *Global Governance and the UN: An Unfinished Journey*. Bloomington, Indiana: Indiana University Press, 2010.

ABOUT THE AUTHOR

Hon. Douglas Roche, O.C., is an author, parliamentarian, and diplomat, who has specialized throughout his forty-five-year public career in peace and human security issues. He lectures widely on peace and nuclear disarmament themes.

Mr. Roche was a Senator, Member of Parliament, Canadian Ambassador for Disarmament, and Visiting Professor at the University of Alberta. He was elected Chairman of the United Nations Disarmament Committee at the 43rd General Assembly in 1988.

Mr. Roche was the founding Chairman of the Middle Powers Initiative, an international network of eight non-governmental organizations working for the elimination of nuclear weapons. In 2010, the City of Hiroshima named him an Honourary Citizen for his nuclear disarmament work and particularly for founding the Middle Powers Initiative.

The author of twenty-one books, his latest is *Peacemakers: How People Around the World Are Building a World Free of War* (Lorimer, 2014). His memoirs, *Creative Dissent: A Politician's Struggle for Peace,* was published by Novalis in 2008. A previous book, *The Human Right to Peace* (Novalis, 2003), was the Canadian Book Review Annual Editor's Choice scholarly selection for July–August 2005. He has contributed chapters to more than twenty additional books.

Mr. Roche holds nine honourary doctorates from Canadian and American universities and has received numerous awards for his work for peace and non-violence, including the Mahatma Gandhi Canadian Foundation for World Peace Award and the United Nations Association's Medal of Honour. In 1995, Pope

John Paul II presented him with a Papal Medal for his service as special adviser on disarmament and security matters, and in 1998 the Holy See named him a Knight Commander of the Order of St. Gregory the Great. He received the 2003 Peace Award from the Canadian Islamic Congress and the 2005 Luminosa Award for Unity from the Focolare Movement, North America. In 2005, he was given Lifetime Achievement awards from both the Canadian Pugwash Group and the Nuclear Age Peace Foundation.

In 2009, he received the Distinguished Service Award of the Canadian Association of Former Parliamentarians for his "promotion of human welfare, human rights and parliamentary democracy in Canada and abroad." He is an Officer of the Order of Canada. In 2011, the International Peace Bureau nominated him for the Nobel Peace Prize.

Email: djroche@shaw.ca
Website: www.douglasroche.ca

INDEX